© Michelle Emerson

This book is sold subject to the condition that it shall not, by way of trade or otherwise, be hired out, lent or resold, or otherwise circulated without the author's/publisher's prior consent in any form of binding or cover other than that in which it is published and without a similar condition including this condition being imposed on the subsequent publisher.

The author has used her best efforts in preparing this book and it is strictly for educational purposes. If you wish to apply any of the ideas contained therein, then the author disclaims any warranties, merchantability, or fitness for any particular purpose.

Any reference in this book to third party websites, materials or methodologies is provided for your information and convenience only.

The moral right of Michelle Emerson has been asserted.

How to Write a BRILLIANT Business Book

4 Simple Steps to Help You Start & Finish Writing Your Business Book – Minus the Overwhelm

Michelle Emerson

Dedication

To all those smart, sassy, go-getting entrepreneurs out there who never give up on their book-writing dreams.

You've got this!

Contents Page

Introduction   1

Step 1 – Time for the Prep Work   8

Step 2 – Creative Juices & Plenty of Planning   36

Step 3 – Get Writing!   57

Step 4 – Sparkle & Shine   81

Bonus Resources   107

Connect with the Author   108

About the Author   114

The Blog Archives   116

Why Read This Book?

1. Because trying to write your business book without guidance never works *(how many times have you started and stopped?)*.

2. Because it leads you gently through each step of the creation process *(without you having to invest hours and hours into research)*.

3. Because it teaches you how to set targets, create realistic deadlines, and carve writing time into your daily life *(without giving up your day job)*.

4. Because it stops you wallowing in Stucksville and stagnating in overwhelm, *(and ensures you reach the chequered flag)*.

5. Because it shows you that writing your book doesn't have to be a gigantic thing on your to-do list *(and that it can be simple when you have a blueprint to follow)*.

6. Because it shares marketing hints and tips about self-publishing, too, and if that's your intention route, you'll be armed with heaps more understanding and confidence to try.

And because once you knuckle down and write your book, you'll bag heaps of business-boosting benefits just like these...

You and your business will get noticed more

With a credible, high quality business book to your name, you'll won't just stand out from the competition, you'll shine. You see, your book is a great culmination of all your hard-earned knowledge. Just think, how long have you been studying, training and developing your skills? Without a doubt your business book will demonstrate you're a true expert in every sense of the word.

You'll grow your fan base

And if you're serious about growing your biz, your book will most definitely help. It will give you more potential to increase your social media followers and your subscriber list, and people who may not have ordinarily found you, will!

You'll feel fabulous

Honestly, you will. There's nothing quite like that feeling of becoming an author – ask anyone who's published their book. It's fantastic.

You'll find new opportunities

I know so many business owners who have been offered new opportunities because of their books. New doors open that were once tightly shut. Your book gives you a rich kudos, and can lead to speaking gigs, both national and international. How exciting would that be?

Why else?

Because I've written this book for you.

I want you to see it doesn't have to feel like climbing a mountain, and it doesn't have to take forever just to get started. It's more about baby steps, bite-sized chunks and daily healthy writing habits to keep you on track.

I want to help you get it written, so you can start working on the sequel… so you can start working on your 'How-to' series… so you can get seen as the go-to expert in your field, and be recognised as a successful and established author… so you can wave your book around at networking sessions instead of your 'oh-that's-so-last-year-dahling' business card.

I don't overcomplicate any stage of this book-creation process.

I don't use jargon just for the sake of it.

I want to help you write your business book as quickly and painlessly as possible, so YOU can reap the author rewards.

I want to help you share your message with the world because I think it deserves to be heard.

Press the **Buy with One Click** button now and let's start your exciting author adventure.

Best wishes,

Michelle

Michelle Emerson

Introduction

Congratulations!

Well done! You've taken an important leap forward today. And that book-writing dream of yours is inching nearer and nearer now that you've invested in this book. So please keep it close by, be determined, stay motivated and create your good writing habits.

In this pre-amble, I want to show you how to use this book to bag the most benefits (instead of just wading in to the 'get writing' part). I'll also explain the ins and outs of this exciting process and elaborate on why writing your biz book can bring you so many exciting rewards.

And if you're prone to mindset wobbles, I'm going to talk about those too. They can be pesky blighters and stand in the way of your author adventure but don't worry. Mindset wobbles are completely normal, I promise. They're just your brain's way of keeping you safe (instead of being all wild and trying something new!).

So, shall we get started? Okay.

Firstly, let me explain how to use this book.

This book is designed to help you get that first 30,000-word draft written in the easiest way possible, and while there's a lot to take in initially, the process is simple.

You would be wise to read the entire book first, and then revisit the chapters one by one, so you know what to expect from each step.

I'd also suggest you familiarise yourself with the topics in The Blog Archives. This way, if you feel like you're succumbing to writer's block, you're procrastinating about time, or you're caving to those Negative Nora voices in your head, you'll be armed with the tools to overcome them.

It's also a good idea to download the sample worksheets I've created for you too. You can find out how to access them on the **Bonus Resources page**.

Many of the questions and prompts and practical exercises throughout this book have been repeated or reframed. This is intentional because I want to encourage you to dig deep when considering your answers. The deeper you can reflect on your answers, the more depth you will bring to your book.

Right, then. Just before we get cracking, let me share a couple of pointers with you.

1. **Your book isn't going to write itself**. No matter how easy I make the creation process for you, I cannot write it. By all means procrastinate, find excuses to avoid it if you must, but once you've got over your tantrum/wobble, take a step back and think about whether it's a good use of your energy. Is it really going to help? Or will it just trap you into *talking* about writing your book but *doing nothing about it?*

2. Once you get into your daily/weekly writing sessions please don't do any editing. At this point it's all about getting that first draft ready. So, **WRITE FIRST, EDIT SECOND** or you'll never reach that final chapter.

3. If you find yourself struck down by an empty creative juice tank, stagnation (in any form) or you can't stop faffing, remind yourself why writing your book is such a great idea in the first place. Here's a story to help...

Picture the scene...

You're reached a point in your business where you can't progress any further, so you're looking for a business coach. You've researched a few potential coaches who look like they could support you. You've asked trusted friends and colleagues for recommendations. And you've whittled down your list to two potentials.

Both are seasoned professionals with an impressive tribe of social media followers, 5* reviews, and websites which capture your pain and promise to solve your 2am panic moments. Each have a shed load of impressive testimonials and require similar financial investments.

But there's one BIG difference.

One of them has written a book about coaching, and the other one hasn't got around to it yet. Does the published author now seem to be more of an expert? Would this sway the decision for you?

Personally, I would envisage the coach who is also an author to have the upper hand here. She's clearly an expert in her field, but she's also got other talents (like writing books, for example) and this demonstrates to me that she's worth investing in. I wouldn't jump straight in and hire her at this point, however, particularly if the financial investment is heavy. Instead, I'd buy her book to see if I can gauge her ethics and determine whether we're a good fit for each other before taking things any further. Once I've read her book, and hopefully built up a connection with her (or resonated with her message), I won't need to go down the long, drawn-out know, like and trust road. Because I'll feel like I already have a clear image of her and her expertise, and I won't waste any more time thinking about whether to hire her – I'll just go for it.

Anyway, back to you and your book (and those pesky potential roadblocks). Like many of my authors you'll have days where the wobbles kick in, the Negative Nora mind chat fires up, and your writing flow diminishes. And no matter how driven, focussed and motivated you are, your own version of the wobbles will creep up at different stages of the creation process.

You'll go from feeling really excited and telling all your closest friends and family that you've started writing your book... to doubting whether you're even capable of putting one word in front of the other.

But if you are aware of what these wobbles are (procrastination/bare-faced excuses/flaky spells/tiredness/writers' block) and create a strategy to overcome them, you will keep up with your writing.

So instead of thinking/saying:

- "I've got too much other stuff to do."
- "I'm rubbish at writing, anyway."
- "I haven't got time to write today."

Reframe these ideas and words into:

- "I can't make my book a priority today, but I will find half an hour to read through yesterday's work/plan my writing tasks for tomorrow."

- "I'm not having the best writing day, but I know it's because I'm tired or too busy with client work to focus properly. But tomorrow's another day, so I'm not going to beat myself up about it."

- "How can I make time to write today?"

If while you're writing your book, or working your way through this one, you find yourself wobbling, or faffing, then bookmark this page. It will give you the motivation and inspiration to pick up where you left off, and hopefully stop you from shelving that book dream of yours. Remember, there are lots of blogs in [The Blog Archives](#) that might help you get back on track, too.

Now let's get started, shall we?

Step 1

Time for the Prep Work

Introduction

Before you can even begin to think about what you're going to write, you need to think about the bigger picture. Even though you might be bursting with ideas and you just want to start writing, without a solid plan in place, you'll have nothing to fall back on when your muse temporarily disappears, or your ideas dry up.

This crucial first step will help you to:

- **get those creative juices bubbling** - you're going to squeeze every drop of your ideas, yes even the crazy ones, out of your head

- **think about what you *could* write about versus what you *should*** - and learn how to cut the magical stuff from the dross

- **research the competition** - and realise why it's crucial to know what's already been written

- **set an intention for your book** - so you always remember 'why' you're writing it

- **and create a vision for your book** so you can focus on it when you're feeling scared and get back on track.

What to expect by the end of Step 1:

By the end of Step 1, you can expect to have a very clear idea of the kind of book you're going to write, what's already been written and published in your field of expertise, what you intend your book to do for your readers, and that all-important big vision.

<<<PRACTICAL TIME>>>

Get those creative juices bubbling

Let's begin with a practical exercise to get your book-writing energy fired up.

Please think about your answers as deeply as possible and write them in the space provided **(or if this a Kindle version grab your worksheets online – full details are on the BONUS RESOURCES page).** Keep your notes safe because you're going to need them for laying your book's foundation a little later.

We're going to start by thinking about your big **'why'**. Having a clear idea about your 'why' will keep you motivated when you're feeling meh and spur you into action when you're struggling to think of what to write.

So, tell me, WHY are you writing this book?

- Do you want to touch people's lives?
- Inspire?
- Motivate?
- Teach?
- Or is it more about realising your own dreams and goals?
- Or spreading the word about your biz to help it grow and build your fan base?

Write as many 'why' reasons as you can...

WHO is your book for?

Think about your ideal reader now - we'll cover this in more detail a little later, but this will help you gain some initial clarity.

- Are your ideal readers also your ideal clients?
- Are your readers stuck in some way and you're going to help unstick them?
- Are they male/female, young/middle-aged/older?
- Do they have jobs or are they entrepreneurs?
- What benefit will they get from reading your book?

If you haven't done so already, build up a profile of your ideal client and see how many similar traits they have with your ideal reader. Don't worry too much about this if you're trying to reach a broad audience. But if you can find an element of clarity, this will help you gauge what kind of language to use, how much jargon you can safely include without alienating some of your readers, what their level of understanding will already be, and that kind of thing.

Having a clear picture of your reader will enable you to know just how to reach out to them, and consequently establish that vital connection once they've finished reading your book.

Use this space to bullet point your ideal reader ideas...

What's your BIG message?

What is this powerful message you want to share with the world?

- Are you going to teach your readers something (eg write your biz book in 30 days)?

- Are you going to inspire them to follow their dreams?

- Open their hearts to change?

- Teach them a new skill?

- What does this entail?

Write down as many keywords about your message as you can. Then mould them into phrases or sentences. Don't worry if it takes a few goes to get this snappy and succinct – the longer it takes the more powerful it will be.

Michelle Emerson

Okay, are your creative juices bubbling now? Are you bursting with ideas and all fired up? Super! Let's keep up the excitement bubbles and get some clarity on your content now... just in case there are still a few hazy bits blurring your book vision.

<<<PRACTICAL TIME>>>

Just Because You Could, Doesn't Mean You Should

Before you can begin your research and writing, you need to pin down the content of your book. You might have no idea as to what type of business book you want to write. You might have more than one book bubbling away. Or you might have so many book ideas that you simply can't choose what's best for your debut. And that's what we're going to tackle here.

There's a saying when it comes to writing – 'write what you know' and this is good advice for someone making their author debut. By all means, pop on those adventurous walking boots once you've written your first book and got it out of your system, but for now, let's keep things easy. I'll give you an example to pave the way...

Let's say you're a therapist who wants to write a business book, but you just don't know what kind of book to write. Let's look at some potential titles you could consider...

1. How to market your therapy business on a budget.
2. From 1-1000 therapy clients in 30 days.
3. A simple guide to setting up your therapy biz.
4. Passive income ideas for your therapy biz.

See what I mean about the different *kinds* of business books you could write? Now if this has set you off on another floodgate adventure, don't panic – I have an exercise to help.

Use the following sheet and create a list of business book types you could write about (like the examples above). Mark them out of 10 as to how much research you'd need to do (with 10 being a ridiculous amount of research and 1 being miniscule). This simple exercise will help you get crystal clear on what your first book should be about – hint, you're looking for content that requires as little research as possible. And if you know you're definitely going to write book two after this debut journey, make sure you keep this worksheet!

How to Write a Brilliant Business Book

Topic	Marks / 10

Now it's time to look at the competition...

Okay, so now you've got your book idea firmed up, it's time to take a look at what's already been written (or not, as the case may be).

If the 'C' word brings you out in hives, please bear with me. Because I know - in a funny kind of way - you're going to get oodles out of this exercise. Honestly!

Firstly, let me explain why you must invest time in researching the competition.

1. You need to know IF there's a market for your book and find out more about it so you can tailor your book accordingly.

2. You'll learn WHAT the 'best-sellers' are and why they're at the top of the leader boards (and how to sprinkle some of their winning ingredients into your book).

3. You'll find out the different kinds of business books that are currently in your field of expertise (and spot any gaps for your book to slot in).

See what we're doing here? It's all about getting that genius little edge over your competition, and making their weaknesses become your strengths.

<<<PRACTICAL TIME>>>

What does the competition look like?

To get a feel for the kind of books that have already been written in your specialist subject area, make your way over to the Amazon Kindle store (even if you don't intend to publish via Amazon Kindle, this is still a good yardstick).

Find the best-selling books which look similar to what you're about to create. You can do this by adding something like 'Business Coaching Books' into the search bar at the top of the page and seeing what comes up. Or you can look through the categories on the left-hand side menu and choose one which has similarities to your book.

Now you need to look at the top 5 books (choose 10 if you want to dive deeper into this section) which pose the strongest competition and answer the following questions as fully as possible.

1. **How is the book title worded?**

    a. Is it a benefits-driven title with a timescale? Eg *Lose that baby fat in 30 days or less.*

    b. Is it a title + sub-title laden with benefits? (Eg Want to lose that baby fat and keep it off forever? or, How to transform your body shape in 1 month without setting foot in the gym.

    Make a note of the titles and subtitles, think about the way they are worded, and which ones pique your interest.

2. **What do the authors focus on?**

    a. Transformation? Eg from Amateur to Pro in 6 simple steps?

    b. Tackling problems? Eg how to start a business on a budget?

    c. Or are they *complete guides to...* or *handbooks* or *workbooks* aimed at specific audiences (eg postnatal mums or entrepreneurial novices or time-poor writers?

Add your findings to your notes.

3. How do these bestselling authors compel their readers to buy?

Read through the book descriptions of these best-sellers. Look at the sales tactics they've used. How do they persuade readers to buy? What kind of hooks do they use to pull in their readers? Do they ask questions or use cliff-hangers to compel them to keep reading? What promises do they make? What do they claim the end result will be from reading the book? What would make you want to buy this book? How does this book stand out from the others?

Create a list of bullet points as you read through the descriptions of your chosen 5 books. By the end you'll have your very own checklist of what a persuasive description looks like – by the way, keep these notes if you're self-publishing as they'll come in handy for your blurb/Amazon description – and you'll have sparked some damn good ideas for scoping out your book, too. We'll get on to that part shortly, I promise.

4. What are the strengths and weaknesses of each book?

Read through the book reviews (if there are any) and write down the strengths and weaknesses of each book. Some reviewers might say, for example, 'I love this book but it doesn't talk about x, y and z and I really wanted to know about that'. So make a note that you need to mention x, y and z in yours. Others might think it was too long, or too short, or too technical, for example. Make sure yours does the opposite and fills the gaps these books have left wide open. And if people pinpoint what they love about the book, add a smattering of something similar (but even better) to yours too.

5. What categories are these books in?

I ask this because sometimes it can mean the difference between getting lost amongst the competition and working your way up the best-seller list. If you've written a book, for example, that's all about hypnobirthing, it may not necessarily sit in the 'Alternative Therapies' category, it may be better off sitting in the 'Pre-Natal Mums' category or 'Birthing' or 'Pregnancy Alternative Therapies'. Finding a niche that you've narrowed down even before you begin to write, means you're already a step ahead of the competition, and it could translate into more impressive royalty payments.

Investing time into researching the competition is something you'll reap many rewards from, so please don't gloss over this section. It could be the difference between starting and finishing writing a viable book that sells.

By the way... I hope you didn't get too sidetracked on your little wander around the Amazon book store. When I did this exercise, I bought two books – almost three but I stopped myself.

So now you've got your content sorted, the competition's finer points nailed, and your book idea is slowly coming to life, let's sort out the last little bit for this section.

Creating a vision for your book and setting an intention

It's a good idea to set an intention for your book and create a vision. Even if you're not a woo-woo kinda person, please bear with me here. It's beneficial to set an intention and create a vision for any new project you're embarking on because:

1. they keep you focused on the end result (and make you realise why you started this project in the first place)

2. they stop you going off on a tangent (which is very easy to do when you're writing just about anything)

3. and they keep you motivated through any wobbly patches (when your inner Negative Nora is having a field day)

Setting a clear intention from the outset means you're much more likely to make choices which are positive and support your end result.

<<<PRACTICAL TIME>>>

Creating a Vision for Your Book

Let's look at your book's bigger picture and make it come alive. Because once it begins to feel real, instead of just an idea, you'll want to work on it as often as possible.

Use these questions to brainstorm an intention for your book. Answer as fully as possible so you can really get to the crux of what your book is going to look like, and more importantly, to help you cater for all those lovely potential readers from the outset (instead of finishing your first draft and then having an epiphany!).

Here goes...

Why are you writing this book?

- Maybe you want to share your entrepreneurial story to inspire others.

- Perhaps you want to transform someone's life/business, while at the same time find new clients, grow your business and boost your profits.

- Or you might want to teach someone a new skill.

In my case, for example, I want to help talented entrepreneurs to write their business books as painlessly and as quickly as possible. I want to share my expertise and knowledge, so they can achieve something incredible, and become the author they've always wanted to be.

Who are you writing this book for?

Think about your target audience in as fine a detail as possible.

- Are they male or female?
- How old?
- Disposal income?

- What do they do for a living?
- Do they work at all?
- Where do they holiday?
- What do they do in their spare time?
- Do they have children?

If you're unsure about your target audience here, take a look at the insights on your business Facebook page. This data provides some very valuable details about the average age and gender of your followers, where they are in the world, their interests, and what time they're mostly on Facebook. If this paints a picture of both your ideal audience (and potentially your ideal reader) you can bear this in mind when it comes to writing for them.

You'll be able to imagine them as you write, which in turn will make your voice oodles more powerful. Furthermore, your message will be heaps more likely to resonate with your reader, because you'll have an uncanny knack for knowing what makes them tick.

In my case... I'm writing this book for small business owners and entrepreneurs between the ages of 30 and 65, who have already achieved a degree of success. They are determined to branch out and take their business to the next level and understand that one of the best ways to do this is by sharing their hard-earned knowledge with the world. I want to help them get established as savvy experts (even more savvier than they already are) and gain their author stripes. I want to help them grow their tribe, enjoy a brand new entrepreneurial adventure, reach out to a new audience, generate more high-quality leads, put their prices up with confidence, and, ultimately, boost their bank balances.

What are your readers going to get from your book?

- Financial benefits?
- A positive difference to the way they live their lives or run their businesses?
- A new skill that they currently have no knowledge of?
- Or are you going to help them stop smoking, yo-yo dieting or squish their phobias?

Think about the biggest benefit your readers will get from your book and write it down (I'll explain why in a little bit).

How are you going to persuade your readers to buy your book?

What makes your book so different from the others in your niche? You need to know what your USP (unique selling point) is so you can stand out from the crowd. Remember what you came up with when you looked at those best-selling book descriptions? Cast your eyes back over those notes if you've forgotten.

If you're still a bit wobbly about this one, then grab your pen and do some brainstorming about your ideal audience's pain.

- What keeps them awake at night?
- What problems would they love to solve if they had the time, money or expertise?
- What skills would they like to learn so they don't have to keep paying someone else to do it for them?

Think about these questions. Then focus on how you can help them (break the process down into its simplest form) and determine why your help is so different or easier to implement or quicker to glean results than anyone else's.

Where are you going to promote your book?

- Online and offline?
- Social media?
- Advertise in a magazine?
- Will you try to garner local and/or national PR – by yourself or with a PR expert?
- Will you share it with your subscriber list?
- Promote it at networking events or speaking gigs?
    - Will you promote it on your website and blog about it?

- Will you add it to your bio with your guest blogs?

Keep all these ideas because you'll need them when the time comes to publish/submit your book to a mainstream/traditional publisher.

When are you going to launch your book?

Without a deadline, nothing ever gets done. So it's important you have a launch date in mind. Be realistic and don't feel overburdened. Put too much pressure on yourself and you'll crumble. Create an achievable launch date and it will keep you motivated and help you build up momentum every week.

Once you've decided on your launch date, you can create regular, daily or weekly milestones and targets to keep you on track. Don't worry if you have to be flexible about your launch date now and again, deadlines are malleable.

What difference will your book make to your business?

That's a biggie, isn't it? Are you looking to add to your tribe, boost your income, open doors to speaking gigs, get noticed by key influencers, shine amongst your closest competitors? Dig deep here. It will help if you think about the emotions your book will evoke on launch day. Write them down.

All done? Okay, great.

Now let's sort that intention for your book...

What I'd like you to do next is to consolidate all the information you've conjured up during this practical exercise and transform it into a **simple intention statement.**

It may look something like this...

"I am writing this book (insert title/working title here) **to help my** (insert ideal reader – eg mums / readers / start-up businesses / teachers / lawyers / web designers) **to transform their** (lives / businesses / wealth / marketing). **It will be launched on .... and it's going to be a huge success."**

It's as simple as that. Think big and think positive here, though. There's no point in creating a watery or flaky vision if you want it to be a best-selling, knock your socks off kinda book. Make your vision bold and powerful. This is your time!

Once you've played around with a few different versions of your intention statement and you're happy with it, write it out and stick it on your pinboard or wall. And look at it every morning when you sit down at your desk, and every evening before you go to sleep. Let your subconscious think about it while you dream.

Having a statement, or creating an intention, for your book is going to keep you focused throughout every stage and wobble of the creation journey. It's going to motivate you when you're questioning your writing skills. It's going to serve as a reminder that you're planning for your long-term business future, taking care of your readers/ideal clients, and it's going to give you clarity throughout the creation process.

If you're into vision boards then why not create one for your book and keep that near your workspace too? Cut out pictures from magazines (can't beat a bit of cut and stick, can you?) and make it gorgeous, big, colourful and bold, just like your statement. Add pictures of your readers, the launch date, the jacket cover ideas and pictures of all the lovely piles of money you want it to attract. And again, look at it morning and night.

Well done!

You've reached the end of Step 1 now, and if you've kept up with the practical exercises and not skimmed through them, you will have already laid a very solid foundation for your book – which means your percentages of finishing your first draft have just skyrocketed.

Before we move onto Step 2, let's have a quick recap of what you've learnt and/or done so far.

- You understand how important it is to do plenty of research before you even start to think about writing.
- You have a clear idea of your book's BIGGER picture.
- You know what your main competition is and how to make their weakness your strengths.
- You understand the benefits of defining your niche.
- You know who you are writing your book for and will keep them in mind as you write.
- Your big, powerful intention statement is now pinned to your wall where you can see it every day.

- Your vision (and/or vision board) is crystal clear and will keep you motivated when Negative Nora fires up.

"When you want something, all the universe conspires in helping you to achieve it."

Paulo Coelho

(taken from The Alchemist)

Step 2

Creative Juices & Plenty of Planning!

Introduction

Now you have your firm foundation and prep work sorted, it's time to unleash those creative juices and bring your book to life. So get your pen poised because Step 2 is all about creating a mind map and unleashing all those fabulous ideas you've been harbouring.

Once you've done this, we'll give your mind map a sparkly new makeover to give it clarity and dissolve any anxt that may be creeping in.

And then we'll get cracking on creating a solid framework for your book, so you are always thinking about the next small step you have to take, instead of getting overwhelmed with the 'Oh, my goodness, I've got a whole book to write' kind of unnecessary drama.

<<<PRACTICAL TIME>>>

The 1st Big Brainstorm

Grab a piece of paper and a pen. (Told you I was keeping it all simple, didn't I?) Put the title of your book in the centre of your paper and place a colourful, big circle round it.

By the way, switch off your phone and any other distractions at this point – we need laser sharp focus here.

Now write down every tiny little scrap of idea that pops into your head. From the biggest branch to the tiniest twig – everything counts... every word, every image, every teeny tiny spark of an idea.

Don't worry about the 'how' at this stage, ie how to write down your ideas, and don't waste time fixing your spellings, or thinking about the jumble of ideas in front of you and where to place them on the paper, or anything else aesthetic. Just let the ideas flow.

Set a 10 minute-timer if it helps you to focus, and maybe a bit of your favourite music to concentrate (usually Ludovico Einaudi for me).

And if you find yourself staring at this sheet of paper thinking, 'Where the heck do I even begin?' then use these prompts. I guarantee they'll open the floodgates.

1. What's your book going to look like?
2. Are you going to include an FAQ section?
3. Who are your ideal readers?
4. What kind of questions are you answering for your readers?
5. What kind of journey are you sharing with your readers?
6. Will you publish it on Kindle or look for a mainstream publisher?
7. How will you change their lives?

8. What are you definitely going to include in terms of content?
9. What are you definitely NOT going to include?
10. How many chapters will you have?
11. Will you ask someone to write a foreword?
12. Will you include testimonials and case studies?
13. Are you going to have a glossary or an index or a further reading section?
14. Will you add an author bio/personal information?
15. How will you structure your book?
16. Are you going to add images/memes to each chapter?
17. Are you going to include any of your articles/blogs to the book?
18. Will your book work through a logical sequence (ie spanning x amount of days or from beginner to pro etc)?
19. Will you include your personal entrepreneurial journey alongside the 'business bits'?
20. Will you be adding any extra bonuses to drive your readers to your website?

When you've finished take a few minutes to look through your mind map. Keep it close by as you go about the rest of your day. Why? Because I can guarantee that now you've opened those floodgates and emptied your brain, you're going to get even more ideas popping in. Just wait and see!

I hope this first exercise has helped you realise that you do have plenty of ideas and therefore, ample content to create a whole book. Maybe at this stage you've surprised yourself at how many ideas you've got. Perhaps you've got another book (or two) in the making!

Makeover Your Brainstorm

Now you've squeezed out all those last drips of ideas, it's time to build on your mind map. Let's get it tidied up and into some kind of order. So, go and grab your original brainstorming sheet now, and some highlighter pens.

What I'd like you to do now is to create a colour code or key for your brainstorm. You can use these categories as a guideline.

- **Colour 1:** use this colour for anything relating to **content** (such as chapter titles, content ideas, etc).
- **Colour 2**: use this colour for structure, and word count.
- **Colour 3:** for any **ideas** you've got which don't easily sit into the other two categories.

- **Colour 4:** use this colour for anything **audience**-related.
- **Colour 5:** use this for any **blog-related** ideas, ie, are you going to add some of your pre-written blogs to your book at the end of chapters? It's something I've used in this book, and it's an invaluable way of offering your reader even more expert advice and insights.

Now you should have a lovely colourful mind map that has much more clarity than your first one. How's it looking?

Fabulous. Let's keep going then.

Creating Your Book's Framework

Now you've got even more clarity over your ideas and you've organised them to within an inch of their life, let's create a framework for your book. This is an exciting part!

Creating a framework for your book is going to help you enormously when it comes to writing. Knowing the structure of each chapter means you'll be able to be productive and positive, and if your ideas dry up on one chapter, you simply pick up with another and return to the original another time. I'll explain more about that shortly.

Now, this is probably going to be the meatiest bit of work you've done so far, but please don't worry. Everything I'm sharing with you here is explained in easy steps and bite-sized chunks. You will reach the finish line with confidence. I'm sure of it!

Before we begin to focus on the framework, I just want to share something with you.

I know you might be desperate by now to get writing (and I don't blame you) but I wouldn't recommend glossing over this section and just diving in. I've designed this formulaic way to write your book because I want to make it as easy as possible for you. It's based on consistency, productivity, keeping things easy, and helping you finish writing your book (not just starting it and giving up at the first glitch).

With a formula, you're much more likely to get an urge to pick up your writing at every opportunity. You'll be keen to keep ticking off those targets, and as a result, you'll sail through those deadlines. Very quickly, once this groundwork is complete, writing your book will become an itch that you won't be able to resist scratching. And I can't wait for you to reach that stage.

You'll need to stay in the flow, too.

If you're a binge-writer and then you write nothing for a few weeks, you're going to lose your thread. This means when you pick it up again, you'll have to re-read what you've already written (because you will have forgotten) and this is such a waste of your valuable time. Daily writing, in little chunks (teeny tiny ones if needs be) will keep you in the flow, and that's one of the secrets to finishing your book.

So, without further ado, let's get on with that framework, shall we? Let's begin by looking at what you need to include in your book.

An Introduction

Obviously, **an introductory chapter** is always beneficial to help your reader understand what your book is all about. If you're unsure what a good book introduction looks like, here are some ideas to mull over:

- You could include an overview of the content/theme of your book.

- You could share an insight into why you've written your book (to help your readers go from a to z, for example).
- You could write a precis of your entrepreneurial journey and how you've reached your present position.
- You could talk about what spurred you into writing your book.
- You could explain the kind of results you hope your readers will get from your book.
- Or you could explain the structure of your book, and the best way to read and digest it to enjoy the maximum benefit/impact.

A Conclusion

You'll also need a concluding chapter. Every book needs a conclusion to tie things up, reinforce ideas and give the reader a sense of satisfaction as they reach the end. Depending on the kind of book you've written your conclusion could more or less write itself, but you can use these prompts if you need more ideas:

- summarise each chapter to show your reader how far they've come on their journey with you
- reinforce your most important points/messages from start to finish
- talk about next steps/further reading so they can continue with their journey

- if you're planning another book as a sequel/follow-on that relates to the same ideal audience, mention this too

And All the Chapters In Between

I'll explain all about the numbers/word count for your chapters very soon, but this is probably a good time to mention a couple of things about the content, too. When it comes to the content of your chapters, they will emerge naturally if you're:

- using pre-written or recycled blogs as the content for your book - the blog titles will become your chapter headings and you'll know how many blogs you're going to include

- following a linear sequence (ie 20 days to...) - however many days/weeks/steps it takes to reach your end result will be the number of chapters you need

- following a logical sequence (ie from start-up to master) that takes them from beginning to end

If your book doesn't have a natural sequence, don't worry at this stage. As we delve deeper into the framework, your ideas will begin to spark.

What Else Needs to Be Included in Your Book?

An **'About the Author'** page is your opportunity to connect with your reader. Pop a photograph of yourself in there, too, because putting a face to a name is always a good idea. You could think about sharing such things as:

- where you live
- your family (including the fur and feathered members too)
- why you're passionate about your biz/your message/your specialist subject
- what your plans are for your next book
- what spurred you into starting your biz
- what the catalyst was for your transformational journey
- what it's like to work with you / the kind of results your clients get from 1-2-1 work with you

A **'Connect with the Author'** page is crucial, too. This is different from your 'About the Author' page because you're going to add weblinks in here. You need to make it easy for your reader to connect with you on social media, visit your website and download your freebies. And, of course, you need to eke out

46

that wonderful connection they've built up with you whilst reading your book.

If you self-publish your book, you could always ask your readers to leave you a review too, and this is the best page to ask.

You can also add in a sneaky little sales pitch at the beginning of your book – like mine **'Why You Need to Buy This Book'.** Adding this to your opening pages (the prelims) is a great idea, particularly if you're going to self-publish your book on Amazon Kindle (because of the 'Look Inside' feature which allows potential buyers to have a sneak preview of your opening pages). What better way to hook them in?

Write a succinct, persuasive and intriguing page that tells your reader why they should buy (or read) your book, the results they can expect to achieve, and who the book's aimed at. If you can grab your readers' attention with a few witty, pithy sentences (and some extra bullet points thrown in for the skimmers) it could mean the difference between someone pressing the Buy Now with One Click and hopping off elsewhere.

Number Crunching Time

Ok, so now you know what your chapters are going to look like, let's take things to the next level. For the purposes of making this whole book-writing journey of yours as easy as possible, you're going to aim to write 30,000 words. This is by no means set in stone, you might find that you write so much more than this or perhaps even less, but this figure means we can scope out each chapter and paragraph (if needs be) and you won't be left floundering at any point.

This is how we're going to break down that 30,000-word count.

Why You Should Buy this Book – this is a sales tactic and therefore it doesn't need to be very long, so let's cap it at 500 words.

Suggested word count: 500

Introduction – this is all about planting seeds in your reader's mind and building up a connection with you (because you want them to finish the book and continue to engage with you online). You also want to build up their trust, so they feel comfortable investing in reading your book. So, with that in mind, let's aim for a word count of somewhere between 1 and 2,000.

Suggested word count: 2,000

Chapters – this is going to be the biggest chunk of your content (obviously) and so it needs to be around the 20,000-word mark. How you split these chapters is up to you – you could write 20x 1,000-word chapters or 10x 2,000-word chapters (or another combination). All you need to bear in mind here is that your chapters should total around the 20,000-word mark.

Suggested word count: 20,000

Conclusion – as mentioned previously, your conclusion can take various forms, but regardless of its content, I'd suggest keeping it around the same length as your introduction. The main objective is to reinforce the journey you've taken your reader on, show how much you've educated them from the first to the last page and demonstrate how much value you've offered in terms of content.

Suggested word count: 2,000

About the Author – again, you want to reinforce a connection with your readers, so they feel compelled to leave you a review, visit your social media pages or website and/or hire you at a later date. It would be a good idea to aim for around the 1-2,000-word mark. If you're struggling however, you could always pop in some of your glowiest testimonials.

Suggested word count: 1,000

Connect with the Author – as well as adding your weblinks to this page, you could always pad it out with a bit of blurb. Here's an example of one I could use to direct people to download one of my freebies:

"Are you struggling to find your funky writing flow? We all go through it. There are times when you love writing and don't want to do anything but write, then there are others when you can't even write a paragraph. So, if you want to create a consistent and happy flow, I've got something that will help. You can sign up here for my FREE e-book: **Find Your Funky Writing Flow: harness your passion, share your message and connect with your crew.** It can help you out of a sticky spot every time."

If your Facebook is your primary social media platform, share your link and talk about the kind of posts you share, and the range of posts, tips, and advice they can expect to find on there. If you have a Facebook Group, share those details too.

Try and make this section around the 500-1,000-word mark if you can. But don't worry if you can't, because chances are you'll have plenty of words elsewhere to tot up your total word count.

Suggested word count: 1,000

Potentially, you could have hit the 26-27,000-word mark by now, based on these numbers. You don't have to be too finicky if you go over or under, just having a word count target to work towards is the main aim at this juncture, as I've already mentioned. Once you begin writing, you'll probably end up with much more than you ever thought you could. And if you haven't, check out the article on **'Adding Some Padding to Your Word Count'** 'in The Blog Archives. If you've gone way overboard, take a look at the **Help! I've Written Too Much!** article instead.

<<<PRACTICAL TIME>>>

Create Your Paper Stash

So now you've got your book framework sorted let's move onto the next exciting bit. For this exercise, you'll need 15 sheets of A4 paper.

Add your chapter title and the word target at the top of each page for:

- why you should buy this book
- introduction
- chapters 1 -10
- conclusion
- about the author

51

- connect with the author

Remember your colourful brainstorm?

It's time to transfer this information onto the relevant sheet of paper. Just use bullet points at this stage – no need to flesh things out/elaborate on them just yet. For everything that was colour coded as content, add them to your chapters. For everything that was to do with your audience, or blogs, or structure, add them to the relevant sheet. Repeat this process for all your other pages and mark off what you've moved across from your mind map.

As you write on each sheet, lots of other ideas will float in. Don't dismiss them. Write them down. And if your ideas dry up for one chapter/sheet, pick up a different one.

Why pen and paper? My reasons for using good old pens and papers for this exercise are simple.

1. When you write with pen and paper (as opposed to typing and looking at a screen) your mind paints a picture (similar to when you meditate). You focus more on your writing, your breathing rate slows down, and what you write becomes more memorable and meaningful. If this is something you'd like to understand more about (it's a fascinating concept) put 'The Zeigarnik Effect' in your search engine.

Michelle Emerson

2. Secondly, using this method means you can take your paper stash wherever you go, and every time you see it your book will be at the forefront of your mind. Sit it on your desk as you work on other projects or when you're doing client work, and even just the sight of it will trigger thoughts and ideas. If you have a sudden epiphany you can grab your paper and add to it instantly, rather than risk getting side-tracked or your fabulous idea vanishing while you're still waiting for your note-taking app to fire up, or you try to find a secure wi-fi connection. I've taken my paper stashes all over Co Durham in the past – skate parks, swimming pools, coffee shops and when the children were really small, I used to be the only mum I knew who enjoyed going to soft play areas. To me, soft play meant I could write or work on my latest project while the little ones burned off oodles of energy. Yes, my mummy halo burned brightly in those days.

I actually wrote a 14-day course once at our local trampolining centre while my two children boinged for an hour with their pals. To this day, I don't know where all those ideas came from – perhaps it was something to do with only having 60 minutes to get it drafted, or the fact that I could see everything clearly in front of me – I work much better with paper than Word docs – I don't know. But I scoped out the entire course, using the method here (I always have a notebook in my bag), and the bones of this course were created there and then, thanks Infinite Air, Durham!

So, yes, this paper method may seem basic and a tad old-fashioned, but it really works.

Get into the habit of looking at your paper stash at regular points during the day, because even just by refreshing your brain with the ideas you've already got, you're encouraging more to seep through.

Once you've got your 15 sheets full of writing, you'll be ready to start pulling together your book and that's exactly what we're going to do next! But first... let's have a reminder of what you've done so far.

- You know exactly how many chapters you're including in your book.
- You know what they're going to be titled.
- You know how long they're going to be.
- You've transferred your mind map / brainstorm makeover onto your paper stash.

- And you've scoped out the bare bones of your book.

How does that feel? I hope you're excited by now because this book of yours is really starting to emerge.

> "Just don't give up trying to do what you really want to do. Where there is love and inspiration, I don't think you can go wrong."
>
> Ella Fitzgerald

Step 3

Get Writing!

Introduction

Yes, you read that correctly… it's time to start writing. I know you must be excited to reach this point (and I bet you thought we'd never get here, right?!) but please, before you dive into writing, spend a few minutes reading through what this step entails, and then I'll hand you the reins.

What's Step 3 all about?

1. **Copy and Paste Pages**: to save you some time and energy, and get your first draft underway, I've created three generic pages for you to cut and paste into your book.

    a. A copyright page.
    b. A 'Connect with the Author' page.
    c. And a 'Why You Should Read This Book' page.

2. **Chapter Mapping:** make sure your paper stash is handy because very soon you're going to be mapping out your chapters – minus the overwhelm.

3. **Targets and Deadlines:** once you're all mapped out and ready to write, you're going to create your very own realistic targets and deadlines (remember we're all about baby steps and bite-sized manageable chunks) to help you keep moving forward every day.

What to expect by the end of Step 3:

1. **Real, tangible progress** – because your targets and deadlines have been set you'll know precisely how many words you're going to write every day / week to get you to the finish line.

2. **First draft success!** Once this step is complete, you'll be well on your way to confidently finishing that first draft.

So, let's get cracking then, shall we?

Copy & Paste Time

As I mentioned in the introduction, I've written some of the more generic pages for you here. All you need to do is copy and paste these sample pages into your book, and tweak them slightly to add your own stamp, that's it. Yes, really! An overview of each page follows, and you can find details of how to download them on the **BONUS RESOURCES** page.

- The **'Copyright'** page – all that needs altering here is the author name on line one and on the final line). This needs to go at the beginning of your book (I'll show you the exact location when we get to the Chapter Mapping section).

- The **'Connect with the Author'** (or 'Connect with Me') page can be tweaked and added to your book.

- The **'Why You Need to Read This Book'** page will need tweaking, obviously, but, again, it shouldn't be too taxing.

Copyright © *<INSERT YOUR NAME>*, 2018

This book is sold subject to the condition that it shall not, by way of trade or otherwise, be lent, resold, hired out, or otherwise circulated without the publisher's prior consent in any form of binding or cover other than that in which it is published and without a similar condition including this condition being imposed on the subsequent publisher.

The moral right of *<INSERT YOUR NAME>* has been asserted.

Michelle Emerson

'Connect with the Author' page for you to cut and paste.

If you've enjoyed the journey this book has taken you on, then let's keep in touch.

You can visit my website: www.

You can find me on each of these social media platforms:

<Add your links to the images for your ebook version and write the web address in full if you're creating a paperback.>

AND if you'd like to join my private Facebook community that's all about (x, y and z), and spend time with like-minded people who are going through the same ***struggles or journey or adventure or transformation*** as you, then you'd be most welcome. Here's the sign-up link to join: www.facebook.com/ETC.

I also send out a weekly/monthly newsletter and you can subscribe to that here: ***<ADD LINK>***

And I have lots of freebies to share with you, too, which might just help you ***<insert benefits of downloading your freebies>.*** You can grab them from here ***<ADD LINK>***.

'Why You Need to Read This Book' page – copy and paste and tweak to suit

- Just setting out in business ***<or struggling with ??? or looking to learn how to... or searching for inspiration to...>?***

- Unsure where or how to begin building your empire? ***<or how to overcome x, y and z without spending a fortune/getting stuck on the way>?***

<Add more pain points here to pad out this page.>

Then this is the IDEAL BOOK for you.

- Follow this step-by-step guide to setting up your business both online and offline *<Insert a brief overview of your book's aim.>*

- Discover how to lay firm foundations for your business from the outset and avoid ALL the usual stumbling blocks. *<Insert your own sentence here.>*

- Learn the basics of marketing *<insert your book details here>* to get your business established and ready to grow.

- *<Add more benefits about reading your book.>*

Told in easy-to-understand, plain English, this book is a valuable resource you can turn to time and time again at different junctures of your business journey *<Insert the journey you take your readers on in your book.>*

Setting up your business *<insert your book details here>* has never been so straightforward and simple.

Grab your copy of **Starting out in Biz the Easy, Stress-free Way** *<insert your book title>* now and invest in the long-term success of your brand-new business. You won't regret it!

Chapter Mapping & Fleshing Out Your Bullet Points

Are you still with me? Excellent. Keep going. You're almost there.

This section is more text heavy than most of the others, but don't let that put you off. As with everything else, these easy-to-understand step-by-step instructions have been fashioned to help you stay focused and productive.

First of all, cast your mind back to when you created your book's framework. Remember that part? Great. Grab your paper stash now – your 15 sheets of A4 with chapter headings/section headings at the top, the word count and your bullet points. If you haven't finished this completely, you'll need to do it asap, because your next task is all about fleshing out these bullet points to create your chapters.

Here's a little reminder of the chapter/section headings and the (approximate) word count just in case you need it:

Chapter / Section	Word Count Target
Why you need to read this book	500
Introduction	2,000
Chapter 1	2,000 – 2,500
Chapter 2	2,000 – 2,500
Chapter 3	2,000 – 2,500
Chapter 4	2,000 – 2,500
Chapter 5	2,000 – 2,500
Chapter 6	2,000 – 2,500
Chapter 7	2,000 – 2,500
Chapter 8	2,000 – 2,500
Chapter 9	2,000 – 2,500
Chapter 10	2,000 – 2,500
Conclusion	2,000
About the Author	1,000
Connect with the Author	1,000
Total Word Count Target	26,500 – 31,500

(Print this chart if you need to and add an 'Actual' column to mark off your progress.)

Remember, these word count targets are approximate and flexible. Don't overthink too much if you're not reaching the target or conversely, if you've gone way over.

So, back to that paper stash. Let's begin with your **'Why You Need to Read This Book'** sheet. The sample page I created for you earlier was just over 200 words, so if you want to elaborate on your version, you could easily bump it up to the 500-word mark. If you've written it already and you're happy with it, however, just leave it as it is for now. Next, take a look at your **'Introduction'** sheet.

How many bullet points have you added to this sheet? Aim for around 10 if possible so you can flesh each one into a 200-250-word paragraph. Let's break it down even further into paragraph numbers now and add a few more ideas for inspiration (assuming you don't have enough already, of course).

Paragraph	**Ideas for Inspiration**
1 – Introduction	Thanks for buying the book – this is what it's about – this is what I'm going to teach you – this is what you can expect by the end.
2 – To get the most out of this book	The best way to use this book is... It's a dip in and out book that doesn't need to be followed in the order it's written... Download the additional worksheets to go with it before you start reading.
3 – Additional Resources	Have you created a workbook for readers to download from your website? Do you have a Facebook group people can sign up to so they can become part of your community before they even begin reading? Will this maximise their results/help them keep going? Keep them inspired or interested or motivated?

4 - Your call	Add your own ideas here. Do you have technical terms which need explaining?
5 - Your call	Do you want to tell the reader about your own journey?
6 - Your call	Do you want to share case studies with your reader so they can see the kind of results your clients achieve?
7 - Your call	Want to mention any mentors / inspiration you have found along the way that may help your readers too?
8 - Your call	Share your passion for your subject here.
9 - Why you've written this book	This is your chance to connect with your readers. Tell them why you've written this book, why you're the best person to write it, and why you want them to avoid the pitfalls/mistakes that you had to go through.
10 - Conclusion	Sum up the intro in a few words and prepare your reader for what's coming up in Chapter 1.

I hope that's helped to break down your introduction. Of course, you might already have it scoped out and you don't want to follow the framework I've presented. And that's fine. But if you haven't, I don't want you to be stuck at this early stage, and hopefully, this should give you the confidence to get cracking with it.

Let's flesh out your chapters now.

As before, each chapter is going to be made up of approximately 10 paragraphs. Each paragraph is going to consist of 200-250 words, so you can reach that target of 2000–2,500 words in total.

Each chapter will have an introduction and a conclusion (use the same content as detailed in the earlier 'Introduction' table if it suits you). So, technically, you only need to have eight ideas/bullet points per chapter to flesh out.

Take a look at your Chapter 1 sheet now from your stash. How many ideas do you have already? If you have eight or more then that's fab. If you don't, then you could think about using the 'Who, What, Where, When, How and Why' prompts and include a Call to Action/Next Steps to get some new ideas brewing. For example, in Chapter 1, when I wrote about the big picture (of writing your book) I could have broken it down into these 10 paragraphs.

Paragraph	Subject
1: Introduction	What the chapter is about.
2: To get the most out of this chapter	Explain how to get the most out of this chapter, ie by reading it in its entirety first, and then going back to revisit the practical exercises.
3: Why	Why the big picture is important.
4: What	What the big picture is (vision, intention, end result).
5: How	How to create your big picture (brainstorm ideas, sample intention statement, etc).
6: Where	Different places to keep your intention statement/vision – office wall, picture of it on your phone or somewhere you'll see it every day to keep reminding you.
7: Who	Who's going to benefit from doing this exercise – mention those who want to race through the content quickly – and people who start things but don't often finish etc.
8: When	When you've written your intention / created your vision (and vision board if you fancy a bit of woo woo), it isn't set in stone, it's malleable and can grow as your book grows.
9: Call to action/Next Steps	So, go and create your vision and your intention right now.
10: Conclusion	Sum up the chapter and prepare readers for what's coming up in the next one.

Now I know our books are going to be completely different, but this framework could help you to breakdown each paragraph, assuming you need this level of help. If you don't and you've got enough ideas of your own, to flesh out your bullet points into a 2-2,500-word chapter, then brilliant. Go for it!

Now let's flesh out your conclusion.

Take a look at your **'Conclusion'** sheet from your stash and see how many bullet points you listed. Again, we're aiming for eight (plus your introduction and conclusion), so if you have enough already then that's fab. If you don't, here are more ideas for you to tweak as you see fit.

Paragraph	Ideas for Inspiration
1: Introduction	You've reached the end – hope you've enjoyed it and getting the results you need and/or you've been able to glean lots of valuable nuggets to implement into your own life/ business. Marry this up with what you talked about in your introduction too.
2: Consolidate Chapters 1 + 2	Recap chapters 1, 2 and 3, and add some next steps for them to take. Avoid simply cutting and pasting any consolidations already written at the end of each chapter,

	use different words or a different format or even bullet points to give them a quick refresher and reinforce your message.
3: Consolidate Chapters 3 + 4	Layout as above.
4: Consolidate Chapters 5 + 6	Layout as above.
5: Consolidate Chapters 7 + 8	Layout as above.
6: Consolidate Chapter 9 + 10	Layout as above.
7: Reminder	Remind them to download your resources, recap the next steps in each chapter, update their workbook etc.
8: Blogs	If you've got a stash of blogs on your website that your readers will benefit from reading, make a list here and put in the web link for them.
9: Coming up next	Here's an opportunity for you to tell your readers what you have in the pipeline. Whether that's your next book or a new programme or a new VIP package. Use this to promote your brand and get people to connect with you.
10: Conclusion	It's time to go out there and do this (eg write your book, transform your biz, implement these ideas: whatever your book message is all about) – wish them luck, keep in touch and watch out for next episode/book etc.

Time to flesh out the final two sections now.

'About the Author'

This is your chance to connect even more with your readers. So you could:

- **tell them your story** – how you started your journey (be it work or personal transformation)

- **explain the catalyst** which made you decide to (set up your business and/or change your habits/mindset and/or helped you overcome tragedy etc)

- **detail some real-life case studies** to show the results your clients have had from working with you (particularly if you've had a client experience the same journey as you're taking your reader on in the book)

- and, of course, **include a few testimonials** here too, if it's appropriate for your book.

Again, you're looking for a good intro and conclusion plus your eight additional paragraphs, so if you need to break this down into an easy-to-follow table (like the ones detailed previously), do so. Keep the process as simple as possible and you'll make good (and consistent) progress.

'Connect with the Author'

Earlier in this section, I gave you a sample page to use but if you want to pad it out a little more, it's fairly easy to do so. Here's a reminder – please tweak this version, if you like it and it's appropriate, to suit your own freebie/lead magnet/specially designed freebie just for people who have bought your book...

> *Are you struggling to find your funky writing flow? We all go through it. There are times when you love writing and don't want to do anything but write, then there are others when you can't even write a paragraph. So if you want to create a consistent and happy flow, I've got something that will help. You can sign up here for my* **FREE EBOOK, Find Your Funky Writing Flow: harness your passion, share your message and connect with your crew.** *It can help you get out of a sticky spot every time you need a hand.*

Just add something like this to your 'Connect with the Author' page with a sub-heading such as: 'Here's a special freebie to thank you for connecting with me' or something similar.

So that's how to flesh out your chapters and other sections. If you find yourself overwhelmed at any point then simply stop writing and go back to basics. Create your own table and break down those paragraphs, just as I've done. It could mean the difference between ploughing on and giving up.

One final piece of advice before you move to the next section...

When you begin writing your book, I would recommend you create each chapter in a separate Word document (as opposed to one single document for the whole book). This way you'll be able to see what the word count is for each one, and it'll be easier to monitor as your chapters grow.

Targets & Deadlines

Now you're almost ready to write (and I know how excited you'll be after fleshing out those bullet points) so I'm going to make this section nice and short and show you how to set word count targets and writing deadlines to keep you focused and moving forward. Here goes...

In order to keep your writing flowing, it's important to write every day; even 200 words is better than writing nothing. Setting daily and weekly writing targets will help you reach the finish line (and a heck of a lot quicker to boot). Here are a few tips to help set your writing targets and keep up the magical momentum.

Tip 1: Decide on your deadline & work backwards

Let's say, you want to finish writing the first draft of your book within a month (without any editing at this stage). You've done all your planning and you've scoped out your framework, you've got your bullet pointed sheets and you know you need to write (roughly) the following:

Task	Word Count	Total Word Count
Why You Need to Read This Book	500	500
Introduction	2,000	2,500
10 chapters x 2,000 words	20,000	22,500
Conclusion	2,000	24,500
About the Author	1,000	25,500
Connect with the Author	1,000	26,500

Let's round that 26,500 up to 30,000 words to make things easy here. Realistically, if you want to write your book in 30 days, you need to ensure you write 1,000 words a day (x7 days a week). No excuses, no faffing, just do it!

If you want to give yourself a day off each week, aim to write 1200 words a day. If you want to give yourself every weekend off, aim to write 14-1500 words a day.

Just in case the panic vibe is starting to sound, please remember that 1 paragraph = 2-250 words. So if you're writing every day (with a target of 1,000 words a day) that is only 4 paragraphs.

And also remember that you have the bones of your content prepared already, and you don't need to add any research time to this.

Panic over… phew! Does that make you feel better? I hope so. Little and often is most definitely the secret.

If you still can't find the time to write four paragraphs a day, then you might benefit from reading through a couple of blogs I've written – you'll find them in The Blog Archives section at the back of the book and they're titled:

1. I don't have time to write my book.
2. Ditch the distractions and get writing.

Tip 2: Track & Monitor Your Progress Every Day

Tracking your writing progress daily is a very motivating tactic. A simple Excel spreadsheet can help you stay productive and it can be laid out as easily as this…

Week 1	Target	Actual	Balance
1.12.2016	1,000	1,000	
2.12.2016	1,000	800	-200
3.12.2016	1,000	400	-800
4.12.2016	1,000	2,000	+200
5.12.2016	1,000	1,400	+600
6.12.2016	1,000	500	+100
7.12.2016	1,000	1,000	+100
Total	7,000	6,900	-100
Balance to carry over to Week 2			+100

Tip 3: Reward yourself every time you hit a target

It doesn't have to be a big reward, just something that will make you smile. It could be a bar of chocolate, a relaxing bubble bath, or a walk. Whatever your reward, just make sure you celebrate your little wins and you'll keep on writing.

Tip 4: If you lose momentum, don't give up

Tomorrow is a brand-new day. You don't give up on a diet because you had a naughty day, do you? So why give up on your book dream, simply because you've let a few days lapse without writing? All you need to do is review your target sheet and carve out a new plan or increase your word count for a few days and start again. No stalling, now. Focus on how far you've come instead of what you've not done. Blips are very much part of your book-creation journey, so don't let Negative Nora take over.

Tip 5: If you've written too much or too little, it's ok

We all have our own writing voice and style. Some of us write ten words when five will do, and others struggle to elaborate. But whatever your problem is, there is always a solution. Check out The Blog Archives at the back of the book for more inspiration:

3. 'Help, I've written too many words!'
4. 'Adding some padding – when you just can't elaborate on your writing'

You've now reached the end of Step 3. You're making fantastic progress, so keep on going. Before we move onto Step 4, let's recap what you've just worked on.

1. You understand the generic pages and have cut and paste (and tweaked where necessary) them into your own Word documents now.

2. Your chapters, paragraphs and sentences are all mapped out, fleshed out and ready to go.

3. You know how to cut back on your word count if you've got too carried away, and...

4. ... you know how to add some padding to boost your word count if necessary.

5. You have all the tips and advice you need to make the writing process easier and your productivity rates soar.

Final points to remember - keep your chapters as separate documents; it's easier to work this way, as I mentioned before. Please don't do any editing at this stage. The goal here is to get that first draft finished.

Now go, get writing!

> "This one step – choosing a goal and sticking to it – changes everything."
>
> Scott Reed

Step 4

Sparkle & Shine!

Introduction

I hope you're still with me here. Congrats by the way, you've reached the final step in your book-creating journey, and I'm thrilled you've stuck with it so far.

In this final step I will guide you through the proofreading and editing processes, so you can turn your first draft into a professional and appealing book. I'll also give you a couple of checklists to ensure you don't miss a thing when it comes to proofing, preening and editing.

And I'll share some valuable info about self-publishing on Amazon Kindle and CreateSpace.

By the end of this final step you'll:

- know how to turn your first draft into one which sparkles and shines
- have a clear insight into self-publishing and all the potential opportunities it brings.

So let's begin with...

The Editing Process

Okay, so your first draft is ready. Fabulous. Now let's get ready to fine-tune it and transform your first raw draft into an irresistible read. All it takes is some light editing. You take what you've done, tweak the most glaring issues, give it a polish, and voila. Remember, we're doing this the painless way, right?

So, what does the editing process entail?

Just like proofreading, you're going to be on the lookout for any sneaky culprits which have slipped through the net (it usually happens to the most seasoned of editors too, so don't worry).

You'll be looking at your use of grammar and searching for typos and spelling mistakes - and you'll need to check through your work line by line.

You'll need to focus on three main areas.

1. Content & Structure
2. Consistency & Clarity
3. Style & Referencing

It's important to leave a few days in between finishing your first draft and starting on the editing. In fact, the longer you can stay away from your book, the fresher your eyes and brain will be. You won't remember each line or paragraph off-pat because you won't be as close to the book as you were.

Content & Structure

The overall objective here is to have an easy-to-read book that does what it says it's going to do. So, if you're taking your reader on a Zero to Web Design Hero in 10 Simple Steps journey, make sure there are 10 Steps and that they're explained in a clear language which caters for even the most basic levels of understanding.

Read your content aloud to check how easily the sentences flow. If they are complex and cumbersome, you'll hear those clunky parts at this point. Long sentences can easily be reduced into two to improve the message. Spotting wordiness and unnecessary sentences (no matter how brilliant they might read) are key to creating a reader-friendly, lucid book which doesn't entail re-reading sentence after sentence to make sense of it.

As well as fulfilling a promise/statement that your book is going to be about x, y and z, the editing process is also an opportunity to double check your content hasn't gone off on a tangent. This can happen (quite easily) but don't worry, this is the point where you can rein it back in. And hopefully, if you've followed your plan and broken down your chapters/paragraphs as we discussed, this shouldn't be too much of a problem.

For example, if your chapter title is, 'How to Go from Walking to Running in 5 Days' but your content talks about the benefits of running versus walking, and you haven't got the five days clearly outlined, revisit this chapter. This may sound basic, but it is so easy to lose your thread. I've done it with blogs before and have had to change the title (rather than rewrite the blog) when I've finished writing and realised my error. It's much easier to switch it round that way.

If it helps, create a checklist of what your chapter needs to include (you might have detailed this in your chapter's introduction or, indeed, if you created a paragraph chart) and rewrite it, ensuring that everything is ticked off by the end.

Another key part of your editing at this stage is to ensure your writing is concise and crisp. Be mindful not to repeat a statement in two consecutive sentences (by expressing it in different words). Try and vary the length of your sentences too and stick to one idea per paragraph.

And if you tend to repeat the same words, phrases and terms, this can get tedious for your reader. One way to fix this is to use a thesaurus (this is a free online version www.thesaurus.com) and find alternatives.

If your book is text heavy, it's a good idea to break it up. You can use bulleted lists, tables, numbered points or images. Or you could add subheadings or emphasise a statement in a larger font. Making it easier on the reader's eye will make for a better reading experience.

And finally… remember to start each new chapter on a brand-new page. Use the CTRL+ENTER key to add a page break the quick way.

Consistency & Clarity

- If you've included any technical terms or jargon in your book, do you support this with an explanation in layman's (or laywoman's) terms as well? Remember who your audience is and their level of understanding. If you need to, add a glossary to the back of your book.

- Try to read through your content as if you were a beginner (assuming you haven't written an 'advanced' book) and simplify any sentences or paragraphs which sound too technical. If you struggle with this, ask a friend/colleague who has a limited understanding of your subject to give you feedback.

- Make sure names, place names, nouns and dates are spelt consistently throughout your book. If you have a niggle that you might have spelt a place name in two different ways, just do a find and replace (CTRL+H) in your Word document to fix it.

Style & Referencing

Any quotations included in your book need to be referenced properly. Whether you do this with a bibliography at the end of your book, or you cite the name, author and date of the book after your quotation, it's up to you. But make sure you reference them in the first instance. If you're unsure how to set this out, take a look at a bibliography in an academic book or check out this website:
http://www.bbc.co.uk/schools/gcsebitesize/dida/managing_projects/copyrightrev4.shtml

You should also think about your narrative, too (your tone of voice). Have you chosen an informal, colloquial, chit-chat kind of narrative? Or is it from a more formal perspective? Whichever you've chosen, make sure your style is consistent throughout. Don't dip in and out of formal writing if it's supposed to be a friendly, conversational kind of book – or vice versa. You'll easily spot any unnatural changes when you read your content aloud.

Editing Checklist

To help you stay on track with your editing, I've created a checklist to work through. Obviously, you can add to this page if you find you need to remind yourself of extra checks.

Does your conclusion marry up with the introduction and the chapter content? (*Check for each of your chapters.*)	
Do your sentences flow naturally? *(Read them aloud and you'll soon find out.)*	
Could you turn one long, clunky sentence into two snappier, more succinct ones?	
Have your chapters stayed on track – ie does the content match the chapter title?	
Do you repeat the same message in two consecutive sentences (but word it in two different ways)?	

Do you use the same words and phrases over and over again? If so, make a list of them and use your thesaurus to find alternatives and CTRL+H to replace them.	
(Add some of your own checks here.)	

The Proofreading Process

Now your editing has been done, it's time for a final proof. While this might seem like an even bigger hurdle than writing the book... and by now you're probably sick of the sight of the bloomin' thing (we all get to that stage)... please rest assured that proofreading doesn't have to be difficult or painful. Promise.

You can get your book looking clean and error-free pretty easily.

A few tips before you begin the proofreading process.

- **Stay hydrated** – keep a glass of water beside you as you work. A hydrated brain is much better for keeping up those concentration levels.

- **Choose your proofreading time wisely** – don't attempt it at night after you've been working all day and your brain is frazzled.

- **Work in timed batches** – set yourself a goal of 60-90 minutes and then stop. Have a little break, make a cuppa, grab a snack, take a walk around the block and then get to your next batch. This will keep you laser focused.

- **Keep a dictionary close by** – you can't always trust the MS Word spellchecker! I regularly argue with it – particularly its queries over apostrophe use!

- **If your punctuation isn't quite up to scratch**, or you struggle with apostrophes or speech marks etc, then source a copy of *The Penguin Guide to Punctuation* or check out the BBC Bitesize website (https://www.bbc.com/education).

- And last but not least, have a read through [The Blog Archives](#) and you'll find '**10 Top Proofreading Tips to Make Your Writing Sparkle**'.

So, let's get started with your proofreading!

Firstly, you're going to divide your proofreading into three sections:

1. **content** – grammar/typos/spelling mistakes
2. **structure** - headers/footers/spacing
3. **everything else** - chapter numbers/page numbers/ images & captions/ index

Secondly, to make this job a whole lot easier I would highly recommend printing out your book.

Print in double line spacing to make it easier on your eye and use a ruler to work your way down each line of text. Before you print it, however, use your F7 key to run a basic spellcheck. This should weed out any simple typos/errors and save you time correcting them.

How to start proofreading your content

- Set a 90-minute timer (or 60 minutes if you're work better in 1-hour batches). Working longer than this can reduce in concentration lapses, and your proofreading eyes won't be as sharp.

- Work your way through the paper copy of your book from beginning to end, reading through the **content only** (ie don't bother with formatting and spacing etc at this point). Read the content aloud so you can hear if sentences sound clumsy or nonsensical and try to keep to a steady pace.

- Use a red pen (it's actually the law to use a red pen for this exercise!) and mark up any typos/spelling mistakes or missing words. For each edit you make, add a little star at the beginning of the line too. This means that when you come to transfer your amendments to the screen, you won't overlook any that have got lost amongst the text (commas, for example, are easy to overlook).

- Keep a piece of paper (a crib sheet) beside you as you proofread and make a note of anything you need to check once you're finished. This will stop you going off to check a place name (or something similar) and losing your proofreading momentum.

Now, let's check the book's structure.

We'll begin with headers and footers. If you've got them centred, just double-check that the left-hand margin is set at zero (sometimes headers sneak in a little tab and you'll find that your headers/footers/chapter headings aren't quite centred). So, watch out for that.

If you're unsure how to set out your header, then you could have your name on the left-hand side and the book title on the right (in italics). You could have your page numbers in the footer, to the left or the right or centred, it's your preference.

Next, you'll need to check that the spacing in your book is consistent.

- Do you have one or two line spaces (returns) after each chapter heading?

- Do you have one or two line spaces before and after an image?

- Does each chapter start on a new page? (It should, by the way – if it doesn't, just press CTRL+ENTER to move it to a new page.)

- Is your line spacing consistent throughout – ie double line spacing or single line spacing (and not a mix of both)?

And finally... everything else.

Check your chapter numbers run on consecutively. You can do this on screen simply by doing a find and replace – this is one part of the proofreading process that IS easier to do on screen). So, press CTRL+F (to bring up your search box). Type 'Chapter' in the Navigation Box and it will bring up every 'Chapter' in your book. Just run your eyes down the list to make sure you haven't jumped from 5 to 7 or something – it's easy to do and simple to overlook if you're not aware of it).

Next, have a look at your images. Are they spaced correctly? Do they have the right caption beside them? And are the captions error-free?

Then give your index/glossary a good read through to ensure there aren't any spelling mistakes, missed words or typos. Don't worry about adding your contents page at this stage and marrying up your page numbers etc, just leave that until the very end.

Okay, that's the proofreading process explained as easily as possible.

To ease the proofreading process, set targets every day. When you sit for your first 60 or 90-minute proofreading session, count how many words you've managed to get through, and set yourself a deadline and daily target from thereon. Just as with the writing process, these targets will really make a difference. You won't do yourself any favours if you try and proofread the whole book in one sitting.

Proofreading Checklist

Don't start proofreading straightaway. Have a break of at least one day (more if possible) between the writing and proofreading process.	
Get a glass of water and set your timer for 60 minutes (or 90 if that's your preference).	
Is your Microsoft Word **dictionary** set correctly – ie, are you using UK or US spellings?	
Do an F7 spellcheck to weed out the minor typos before you start. (Remember to keep a 'real' dictionary nearby too in case you need to double check anything.)	
Now go through your work (paper copy if possible) line by line with your red pen and ruler, following the three sequences previously outlined.	
Transfer any changes to your Word document and tick them off as you go.	
Repeat the F7 spellcheck process again.	

Congratulations! Now what?

Now that you've got your business book ready and polished to perfection, you're probably wondering what the heck to do with it.

Well, if I were you, I wouldn't hesitate to self-publish. This Indie Author Revolution that has emerged over the past few years has been the best thing ever for aspiring authors. Obviously, however, as with everything else in this world, self-publishing has its pros and cons – let me explain...

Self-Publishing on Kindle

Self-publishing has undergone a huge revolution over the past few years. Aspiring authors can now take control of their writing destiny and become independent publishers, thanks to the likes of Amazon Kindle and its sister print-on-demand platform, CreateSpace, and many more.

Once over, authors had much fewer options. They would either have to spend months or even years, searching for literary agents and/or mainstream publishers (and waiting for them to respond). Or, if they were financially well-off, they could use what was known as 'vanity' publishers and pay thousands of pounds to have their books published, with little chance of recouping their investment.

Thankfully, the number of links in the publishing chain have been reduced and the fat cats of the vanity publishing world are nowhere near as well-off as they once were, say, ten or fifteen years' previous.

The Pros of Self-Publishing

- You have full creative control over your book.
- There are no hefty payouts for 'middlemen' ie agents and publishers.
- You can be in charge of your writing destiny and keep on writing and publishing as many books as you like.
- You can receive up to 70% royalties on each book sold (Amazon keep the other 30% for providing the publishing platform and delivering the digital downloads to your buyers).
- Self-publishing can create a lucrative passive income stream for you.
- Your book can be distributed all over the world.
- It's free – if you are prepared to learn how to format and upload your book.
- It's quick – it only takes up to 48/72 hours for Amazon to approve your book, and then it can be available to the book-buying world.
- Self-publishing can have a huge impact on your business.
- It's exciting!

The Cons of Self-Publishing

- The biggest struggle any indie author (independent author) faces is selling their book. If you want to ensure consistent book sales, you'll need a good marketing plan in place.

- Unless you're a seasoned writer, editor, proofreader, graphic designer and tech whizz and you have some copywriting knowledge, you might easily become overwhelmed with some or all of the necessary self-publishing requirements. But there are lots of people (like me) out there to provide these services for you.

- If you want to be a consistent and long-term indie author, it will pay you to invest in learning how to create, format and upload to the Kindle and print-on-demand platforms.

- Competition can be fierce.

If publishing your book on Kindle is something you're interested in, pop over to The Blog Archives and read at your leisure. They may answer some of your questions, and/or spark new ideas for you.

The Kindle E-book Checklist

If you are going to publish on Kindle, here's a checklist of everything you need to do once your book is ready.

- open a **KDP account** (kdp.amazon.com)
- create your **jacket cover** (using a stock photograph + Canva makes the whole thing very easy)
- write your book's **description** (your back cover blurb on a print book) – the limit is 4,000 characters/700 words
- **keywords** – select seven keywords that potential readers would use to search for your book
- **categories** – choose two of the most appropriate categories for your book (make them as niche as possible and avoid the 'General' categories)
- **price** – decide on a price for your book (check out what the competition are selling for, don't undervalue your work and don't be too ambitious/expensive either)
- **distribution** – decide whether you want to publish all over the world or just in specific countries
- once you upload your book to Amazon Kindle for approval, you should receive a 'Congratulations – your book is now for sale on the Amazon Kindle store' email within 12

hours if you're in the UK (and to be honest, it's usually less than 12 hours).

A Brief Overview of Amazon's CreateSpace

CreateSpace is Amazon Kindle's sister company and offers a free print-on-demand service. This means that if you decide to offer an e-book version of your book (ie Kindle) and a physical copy (ie via CreateSpace) you can have them both for sale on your designated shelf in the Amazon store.

This enables you to potentially double your reach (some people prefer electronic to physical books and vice versa). The process is relatively simple but it's important that you either research thoroughly how to format/typeset your book so that it doesn't look amateurish, and you have a professional-looking jacket cover designed too.

The CreateSpace Checklist

If you want to publish a physical book using CreateSpace, the checklist is very similar to the Kindle one.

- open a **CreateSpace account** (createspace.com)
- create your **jacket cover** (use the cover creator from CreateSpace to make the whole thing very simple)
- write your **blurb** to go on the back of your jacket cover – keep it short, snappy and persuasive (pick up a book and see what a good blurb looks like)
- **write your book description** (you can use the same as you did for your Kindle book)
- **keywords** – select five keywords that potential readers would use to search for your book
- **categories** – choose one appropriate category for your book (make it as niche as possible and avoid the 'General' categories)
- **price** – decide on a price for your book (NB: CreateSpace will tell you the minimum price you can sell the book for – based on the printing costs they determine - but you can decide on the maximum)
- **distribution** – decide whether you want to publish all over the world or just in specific countries

- once you've uploaded your book to CreateSpace for consideration, they usually take 24/48 hours to approve it, then it can take a further 72 hours to appear on your Amazon bookshelf.

The Final Word

By crikey, YOU DID IT!

I hope you've enjoyed this book, and of course, writing yours. I'm thrilled to have been able to support you through this exciting adventure, and I sincerely hope you've enjoyed the process and you're super proud of your achievement.

If you intend to follow-up your debut book with another non-fiction read, then this blueprint will be a great tool to help you again.

You now know those 4 important steps to writing your book, minus the overwhelm. And I'm sure that now you've got this first book written and out of your system, the whole creation process won't seem half as scary as you first imagined.

By way of a thank you for buying my book, I'd love to support you further by sharing details of your book (once it's published and available for sale) on my social media platforms, and with my email subscribers. You can find out how to get in touch with me about this on the **'Connect with the Author' page**.

And all that's left for me to say is good luck with your book and keep up the great work!

Michelle

> "You don't write because you want to say something, you write because you have something to say."
>
> F Scott Fitzgerald

Bonus Resources

As mentioned throughout the book, I have created a PDF of the charts, checklists and worksheets for you to access.

You can find them all here:

https://www.thewritersassistant.co.uk/bonus-resources-write-brilliant-business-book/

when you reach this page, add

!BIZBOOKAUTHOR2018!

into the password request box.

If you have any problems with this, please message me via the contact page on my website: www.michelleemerson.co.uk

Connect with the Author

Want to keep in touch and keep up the writing and self-publishing conversation? That would be fabulous!

Come and say 'hi'!

- www.michelleemerson.co.uk
- https://facebook.com/thewritersassistant2013
- https://www.linkedin.com/in/thewritersassistant/
- https://twitter.com/TheWritersAsst

If you'd like to download some of my freebies and sign up to my newsletter, you can find all the info here:

https://michelleemerson.co.uk/freebies/

If you'd like to work with me on your next writing project, then I'd love to be part of that, too. There are lots of ways I can support you: from ghostwriting and book mentoring, to proofreading, copy-editing and self-publishing on Amazon Kindle & CreateSpace.

Michelle Emerson

And if you're wondering what it's like to work with me before you even think of getting in touch, then have a look through these testimonials from just a snippet of some of my fabulous authors.

Keely Anna Potts reviewed Michelle Emerson Painless Online Publishing — 5 star

December 9, 2017

"Thank you from the very bottom of my heart for all of your help, motivation and patience with me whilst writing Greg Said. You are an angel and it's been an absolute pleasure working with you. I can't recommend you highly enough. Thank you for everything."

~Keely xoxox ♥♥♥♥

Michelle Emerson

Danielle Drozd reviewed Michelle Emerson Painless Online Publishing — 5 star

February 6, 2017 ·

"Michelle edited my debut book I Have a Dream. It was a daunting experience to publish a first book, but Michelle brought a calmness along with her expertise. I knew my book would be in good hands! Thank you, Michelle for taking care of my work and bringing the changes it needed. Would highly recommend Michelle."

Cassie Farren, Author of *The Girl Who Refused to Quit*, and *Rule Your World*

"It is such a personal experience to share your book with someone for the first time. I trust Michelle 100% but still felt nervous as I awaited the edits of my new book. I needn't have worried as when I read through them I loved my book even more. It has made a big difference to know that I have Michelle's support combined with her expertise. I would highly recommend Michelle to anyone looking for a book coach."

Kate Spencer, Practical Spirituality Coach and Author of *Twelve Lessons, Twelve Lessons Later, Twelve Lessons The Journal* and *Walk-In*

"...Michelle has the highest possible standards and this shines through in her work which is certainly top notch. Very highly recommended and I would not go anywhere else from now on as I doubt you could get a better service."

About the Author

Michelle lives in a beautiful little nook in Weardale, Co Durham, England, with her two children, husband and fur baby, Shih Tzu, Buddy.

She's been passionate about writing and reading since the age of 7 when Father Christmas surprised her with a Victoria Plum Secret Diary and has worked in the publishing industry (wearing many different hats) for 20+ years.

And she still has spells where she can't believe she gets paid to write and support authors through their own book-writing adventures.

Michelle Emerson

If she's not locked in her writing cave, you'll find her walking up and down the rolling Weardale hills or hiking through Hamsterley Forest (usually with a notebook and pen sticking out of her back pocket).

The Blog Archives

I've included this additional section to give you even more insights into writing your book and self-publishing, and help you overcome those pesky roadblocks that stand in your way.

I hope you enjoy them.

You can find heaps of other articles here, too: www.michelleemerson.co.uk/blog

Michelle

1. Ditch the distractions and get writing.
2. I don't have time to write my book.
3. Adding some padding – when you just can't elaborate on your writing.
4. Help I've written too many words!
5. Recycling your content.
6. 10 proofreading tips to make your writing sparkle.
7. 5 book-writing blocks & how to ninja kick through them.
8. Thinking of publishing on Kindle? 6 reasons why you simply MUST do it!
9. How to make money by publishing on Kindle.
10. How to Get Your Book Noticed on Kindle.

DITCH the distractions and GET WRITING!

It's all too easy to get stuck in the vicious cycle that is, 'I've really got to write today but...' isn't it? So, if you're having that kind of day and you want someone to get you out of your funk, da-da! Here I am. Enough of the procrastination. That book/blog/fabulous content isn't going to write itself now, is it?

Set a timer

Use an online timer or your phone or an app like Pomodoro and write, write, write.

Make writing a daily habit

Even if you can only fit in 30 minutes per day, 30 minutes is better than 0 minutes.

Focus on one project at a time

Trying to write when you have Mexican jumping beans in your head (throwing ideas around for other projects) isn't going to help you focus. So, keep your focus on the most pressing project and forget about the rest.

Switch off the internet

You really can manage for short bursts of time without having the internet on. And without emails and social media posts/messages dropping in constantly, your writing will flow and your productivity will soar.

Don't listen to your inner saboteur

Your inner saboteur may try to distract you once you get into writing mode but just ignore it. If you have to, thank it for its feedback and tell it you don't have time to listen to it right now because you're busy writing some incredible content instead.

Write first, edit second

You'll never get anything finished if you start editing while you're writing, so try to get into the habit of writing first and editing second. They are two separate beasts and should never be tackled at the same sitting.

Bite-sized pieces

If you've got a BIG writing project to get through, and you tend to get overwhelmed, break down the tasks into bite-sized chunks. You could have mini tasks such as research, reading, and writing 500 words, and once you start ticking off that list, your motivation will grow and your procrastination will diminish.

Leave your phone in another room

Yes, this is something I have to do. How did you guess? Separate your hand (and your concentration) from your phone and put it in another room so that you physically have to stand up and get it if you need a quick check on your emails/social media. It's amazing how just this little interruption to your brain will stop you from reaching for your phone.

Peace and quiet / background music

Some people need have complete peace and quiet to write, others prefer background music. But whatever your preference is, do that. The more conducive your atmosphere is to writing and concentrating, the more writing you'll produce.

Daily target

If you're working towards a deadline and you end up doing nothing at all until you're almost running out of time), then set yourself a daily writing target and do it, no matter what. Make it small to begin with but make it daily and you'll get the results you need.

I Don't Have Time to Write My Book!

Writing your book isn't going to happen overnight, you know that. But it's important to realise that you're not going to magically find time to write your book either.

What you need to ask yourself here is: 'How can I MAKE time to write my book?'

Here are my 5 top tips to help you do precisely that.

1: Get delegating – if you're going to carve out regular, quality writing time then something has to give. So, delegate. Could someone help with your chores? Could you outsource any work-related tasks to a VA for a few weeks? Could you hire someone to help write your book (or do the editing or research)?

Remember, you're not Superwoman/man, (despite your brilliant impression). So, don't beat yourself up about the whole 'asking for help thing'. It is a temporary solution and the more time you can devote to it, the better the results. Remind your inner chatterbox of this if it clambers onto its soapbox. You're prioritising your writing over the regular stuff and this is great.

2: Which leads me smoothly to my next point – **prioritise your writing.** For once, try and forget your usual habits, ie popping up to make the beds when you get back from the school run, or putting in a load of washing before you can focus properly on work, or just making another cuppa before you switch on the laptop. I know the inner chat might pipe up but remember this mantra, **"what you prioritise will progress"**. And right now, your writing needs priority.

3: Get up an hour earlier and just write.
Don't check your phone, don't turn the internet on, just write. (Obviously, grab yourself a cuppa – I would NEVER recommend trying to write without a steaming hot brew on your desk.) If you can write for this whole hour, without stopping to edit/backtrack, your productivity levels will grow day on day and week on week. And that first draft will be ready before you know it.

4: Flex that writing muscle as often as possible. Stop faffing around on Facebook (in the name of 'work') and losing a whole hour (how does that happen?) that could have been spent so much more productively. Cut back on your client appointments if you can, scale back your diary so it's full of writing slots. See that cancelled discovery call as a gift from the universe and get flexing.

5: Dictate your book – some people are natural speakers, others prefer to write/type their words. So, if you're a better speaker or storyteller, than you are at writing or typing, why not try dictating your book? You could get a transcriptionist to type it up and then you could pass it on to an editor/ghostwriter to add some sparkle for you.

Remember there will never be a right time to write your book. Productivity and prioritising are key to making progress. And if that fire in your belly is strong enough, you'll easily find the time to write your book

Adding some Padding When Your Word Count's Too Low

If you've reached the end of your first draft, or thereabouts, and your word count isn't quite what you thought it was going to be, here are a few ways to add some extra padding.

- **Client Case Studies** – people love to read about the experiences others have had, and if you can show you've helped someone overcome challenges or enabled them to improve their business (or even their lives) in some way, this will bring your book to life. Furthermore, the benefits of including case studies will ripple right through the rest of your business too, because when your readers connect with you more and more, they'll be much more likely to consider working with you. Add your case studies to every chapter if you have an abundance of them.

- **Chapter Summaries** – finish each chapter with a chapter summary sheet of what you've talked about or even an action plan if they need to be productive.

- **Next Steps** – add some Next Steps to help your reader take action. This will add more value to your book and give it that all-important extra padding.

- **Top Tips** – add a few top tips at the end of each chapter which summarise the chapter's theme. This will keep your readers motivated and remind them of the key points in the chapter.

- **Additional Resources** – add web/media links to further reading that can help your readers embark on their own research and/or delve deeper into something you've discussed in the chapter.

- **Foreword** – if you haven't done so already, you could consider asking a mentor/coach/past client or colleague to write you a foreword. It's another valuable addition to your book which will extend its length but, more importantly, it will give you an opportunity to shine. If you're a modest soul, you'll probably avoid telling your readers about your incredible expertise and how amazing you are, but whoever is writing your foreword won't hold back.

- **Commonly Asked Questions** - you could also add a Commonly Asked Questions or FAQ section in your book, particularly if you've written a How-To Guide or you're educating your audience in some way. This will pad out your book well, give you even more kudos and provide valuable solutions for your readers, who may then go on to leave you a fab review.

- **Inspirational quotes** – another good addition to your book. They can be used to motivate and inspire your readers, and definitely serve as good padding, particularly if you use them in each chapter and then donate a paragraph to looking at the quote in more detail and/or making it relevant to your book and its message.

A word of warning about padding out your book - don't go overboard just for the sake of it because your reader will see through it. Only add padding if it's genuinely necessary and make sure it's always 100% valuable content that you're adding.

Help! I've written too much!

Don't panic! I, too, suffer from this using 10 words when 4 will suffice thing. And whilst it's often a hard habit to break, you will need to hone your writing style and your message if you want readers to read to your last page.

To begin, let me share a few words you could easily cut out of your vocabulary.

- **'That'** – when I'm editing books for my authors/entrepreneurs this is a regularly overused word. Sometimes it can appear 3, 4 or 5 times, just in one sentence, and it makes for clunky reading. Read through some of your content now and see if you have overused 'that'. Then try deleting the word and re-reading the sentence. 99% of the time, the word is surplus.

- Similarly, if you drastically need to cut back on your word count, you can delete these words, too, or at the very least reduce the amount of times they're used: *really, very, just, then, start, certainly, probably, so, and because.*

- If you want to delete these words or reduce their usage, simply press CTRL+H to open up your 'Find and Replace' options in Word.

Instead of pressing the 'Replace All' option, go through each one to ensure it doesn't impact on the context of your sentence first.

Have you culled these 'surplus to requirements' words? But you're still struggling to reduce your word count? Here are a few more tricks to consider...

Try reading your sentences/paragraphs aloud and ask yourself:

1. Are you repeating yourself in two consecutive sentences (but using different words)? If so, cut out one of the culprits.

2. Do you 'go around the houses' to make your point? Reading your content out loud will help you identify the parts where you're blathering.

3. Is there a clear purpose to every paragraph/sentence you've written? If it's more about artistic license (and your love of words) then sorry but you'll have to press that delete button.

4. Could 5 words be used in that particular sentence instead of 10?

Michelle Emerson

Hopefully, this little exercise will have helped you become more aware of how you write, as well as how to be brave and give your writing a declutter.

Recycling Your Content

Okay, so you've pencilled some writing time into your diary... you've got a nice, hot brew in front of you, and you've opened up a blank Word document.

And nothing.

No muse... no creative juices... not a spark of an idea.

So, what can you do?

Keep staring at a blinking cursor?

No, you just need to look at your content archives. If you've been in business for any length of time and take your content marketing seriously, you'll already have stacks of writing that can easily be recycled.

Blogs

Take an amble through your blog archives, what have you got in there? Did you even realise you'd written so many?

What kind of titles are jumping out at you? Do they fall into natural categories that could form chapters? Or are they full of 'How-tos' that could be used to answer your ideal clients' burning questions?

E-books

Have a mooch around all those freebie e-books you've written over the years, could you pad them out? Breathe some new life into them? Turn them into a workbook? Could you change your 30 top tips to 99 top tips?

Free Challenges

You know all those challenges you created? What could you do with them? Could you transform them into a practical, step-by-step guide or handbook? Or could you add a few case studies and testimonials from the people who completed your challenge and add a little layer of extra value/padding?

Podcasts

If you prefer creating podcasts to blogging, then take a look through your podcast library and think about turning your voice into words. Save yourself time (and possibly a headache) by hiring a VA or transcription company to take care of this for you.

Webinars

Think of how many webinars you've done over the years. Could you turn them into a book?

And there's more...

Look at your social media posts and your client testimonials. Look at your autoresponders which answer generic questions for potential new leads. Think about all the clients you've helped over the years. Can you share their success stories in the form of case studies?

Are you surprised yet?

I thought you might be.

Now, if you're thinking, 'Yeah, I really do have oodles of content... yippee... but what do I do with it', keep on reading.

You've got to think of putting them in an enticing bundle so your potential readers will fall over themselves to buy.

Here are some examples:

- If you're a marketing guru, could you put together a Q&A book based on 50 of your ideal customers' biggest challenges?

- If you're a business coach, could you collate your blogs and take your readers on a journey from start-up status to 6 figure success?

- If you're an online business manager or VA, could you combine all your articles about outsourcing into an 'Everything You Need to Know About Outsourcing' guide?

- If you've started your business from scratch and you're now really successful, could you write a book about your journey and the pitfalls you overcame?

- If you're a therapist, could you write a book about how to market your therapist business to get quick results?

Here are a few more potential titles to help you brainstorm – just fill in the blanks:

- how to ...
- how to be a ...
- 10 ways to fix ...
- what to do when you're a ... and you're stuck
- why you need to ...
- the truth about ...
- debunking the ... myth
- where to find inspiration when you've lost your mojo for your biz
- 6 ways to stop ... and start ...
- 50 reasons why it's good to be ...
- Taking your ... biz to the next level
- why being an entrepreneur (or coach or therapist etc) is the best job ever

And if you're still stuck for ideas at this point, take a look around the Amazon Kindle bookshelves to see if you can spot any gaps in the market. Maybe you could write a similar book to those ones that are already out there but put your own spin on it or write it from a totally different perspective.

As long as you're writing about what you know and love, then creating an appealing and credible book is going to be so much easier than you think.

> *"Don't reinvent the wheel, just realign it."*
>
> *Anthony J D'Angelo*

Michelle Emerson

10 Top Proofreading Tips to Make Your Writing Sparkle

Proofreading your content is a crucial step in every publishing journey.

Since you only get to make that first impression once, you've got to make it the best it can possibly be. Poor spelling, grammar and formatting, gives your audience the impression that you are unprofessional, lack an eye for detail or you're simply too slapdash to care.

Not great, right?

So here are my 10 Top Proofreading Tips to help you show you're a true pro.

#1 Spellchecker

Using your spellchecker is a great start – but don't trust it too much. Make the spellchecker your first port of call because it will pick up on lots of typos. However, there are still plenty of mistakes that aren't picked up by the spellchecker. So, don't assume your work is error-free just because you've used the F7 key.

#2 A Second Pair of Eyes

Ask someone else to read your text. A friend, colleague or family member can spot mistakes that your eyes glance over. Ideally, try and ask a fellow writer or a bookworm; they'll be more inclined to help.

#3 Read It Aloud and Slowly

By reading your work aloud and at a slow, controlled pace, your brain is less likely to auto-correct mistakes. You'll be more likely to find missing words, get a better feel for the flow, and see if you need to step up your punctuation.

#4 Work from a Paper Copy

Reading from paper is much easier than working from your computer screen – and it's better for your eyes and your concentration. And you get to use a red pen and play teacher (or is it just me who likes doing that?).

#5 Use a Ruler & Check Line by Line

The key to catching every mistake is to work slowly and focus on each word and line fully. One way of doing just that, is to take a ruler and go through your text one line at a time. Another is to read from The End and work backwards.

#6 Keep it Consistent

Make sure the way you spell words, names, places etc are all consistent in your text. Is your formatting consistent? Do your chapter headings use numbers or words and are they all the same?

#7 Do Several Separate Proofs

Sorry to break the bad news but proofreading your work isn't just a one-round-and-you're-out process. First you should focus only on your spelling. Next look for any inconsistencies, then check your formatting, and double-check those chapter headings.

#8 Partner Up with a Proofreading Pal

Working with someone else makes the proofreading process much easier. So, grab a pal, and maybe a cup of tea and some really nice biscuits (bribery will be required at this stage – so you should go all out for choccy Hob Nobs) and get started. Let one person read aloud while the other person follows with their copy. This way, any missing lines or paragraphs or mistakes will be much easier to spot.

#9 Check That Your Chapter Numbers Are in Sequence

During the writing process, you may have fallen out of sequence or added new chapters and/or paragraphs at a later date. So, it's important to make sure your chapter numbers haven't gone skewwhiff. An easy way to do this is to use the Find and Replace tool in Word (CTRL+H) and just search for the word 'Chapter'. You'll be able to do a quick check down the navigation menu from there without it all getting too cumbersome and time-consuming.

#10 If You Work from a Screen, Zoom In

If you are working from your screen, rather than on paper, increase the zoom size. It makes it much easier to focus on each line individually.

5 Book-Writing Blocks & How to Ninja Kick Through Them

As entrepreneurs, writers and creatives, we regularly have to face and blast through writing blocks. It's all part of the ride.

Sometimes these obstacles put a ceiling on our success. Others play tricks with our minds (and collude with our inner critic) to diminish our confidence. And often they steal our creative juices and laugh at our struggles to reignite the flow.

One thing all these writing blocks, obstacles, and roadblocks have in common though, is that they all stem from fear. And fear likes to keep us stuck.

To demonstrate, here are a few fears and my expert advice to blast your way through them.

Fear 1: What if nobody wants to read my book?

A frequent (but unsubstantiated) obstacle for lots of writers. Inner critics pipe up with the same old stuck record, 'Who do you think you are? Why will people listen to you?' Blah, blah, blah.

So, to blast this (unsubstantiated) fear to the back of beyond... remind yourself of the billions of people in the world, and that potentially, even a portion of these people reading your book is possible.

Fear 2: There's too much competition.

Yes, it's a noisy, busy world out there with everyone vying for attention. There may be other books out there with a similar title to yours, some which look as though they're trying to attract your ideal reader and some that might even focus on similar content...

But... you can still dropkick this fear to Timbuctoo! Accept that there is competition out there, but realise that they won't have your sparkling personality, your inspirational message and they won't speak in your unique, witty voice. And that's what's going to make your book so unique and inviting. To quote one of my favourite Dr Seuss quotes, remember that...

"TODAY YOU ARE YOU, AND THAT IS TRUER THAN TRUE. THERE IS NO ONE ALIVE WHO IS YOU-ER THAN YOU."

Fear 3: I don't really know what to write about.

Sometimes this can be a pretty big roadblock. When the creative juice tank is empty, but you still feel the compulsion to write your book... but you don't know if it's what people are looking for and so you just put it on the backburner again.

Okay, let's ninja kick this fear right now! If Fear 3 strikes, ponder on these few questions:

- what are you passionate about?
- what gets you out of bed each day?
- how can you change lives?
- what can you teach people to do?
- how can you best inspire people?
- what do you know inside out and back to front that you could write for hours about without doing any research?

Get brainstorming and your book's purpose will emerge.

Fear 4: I'm not motivated enough to finish writing my book.

That's okay, you're human. We are struggle sometimes. Writing is something that's usually done in isolation, so it's only natural that with no one to answer to or even speak with about your book, your motivation levels might wane.

But I know how to fix this fear! Find yourself an accountability buddy. Who do you know who is writing their biz book? Could you pair up with an entrepreneurial friend and exchange motivation sessions?

Fear 5: What if I fail?

That's okay, you're human. We're all scared of failing. Leaving our comfort blankets and blasting through the next roadblock fill us all with fear. But fear is only trying to protect us. Fear is only saying to us, 'Look, let's just stay where we are, we're happy here, it's warm, it's cosy. Why bother with all that?'

So, to blast through this roadblock, remember that failure isn't a weakness, it's an experience, and usually part of the ride when you embark on anything new. It's what helps us get even better at what we do. It's what helps us refuel that fire in our bellies and makes us realise how much we really want something. But be mindful, too, that failure isn't the only option. You can actually fly. Savour these lovely words from Erin Hanson, a young Australian poet...

Michelle Emerson

"There is freedom waiting for you,

On the breezes of the sky,

And you ask, 'What if I fall?'

Oh, but my darling, what if you fly?

And finally,... when your fears are getting the better of you, remember this acronym:

F False

E Expectations

A Appear

R Real

If you're thinking of publishing on Kindle, here are a few specific articles to help enhance your knowledge of what's involved, the benefits, and how to make Kindle work for you.

Thinking of Publishing on Kindle? 6 Reasons Why You Simply HAVE to Do It!

If you've written your book but you're not quite sure what to do with it, my advice, every time, would be to self-publish on Kindle.

Over the years, I've proofread and edited some fantastic books that have literally only been seen by the writer and me. Because the author doesn't feel that publishing on Kindle is for them, they leave their brilliant book languishing in a dusty drawer or hidden away in a desktop folder.

Their long dream of writing a book has been fulfilled and when they receive the finished edited/proofed version, they're usually blown away by how far they've come.

But then the excitement dissolves quicker than a snowman in the sun.

They aren't prepared to go down the self-publishing route – for whatever reason – and I think it's a real shame.

Some writers will try the mainstream route but get deterred and frustrated by the lengthy, drawn-out process, and then they decide that if they haven't been snapped up by a leading publishing house (and quickly) that their work must have been rubbish anyway. In fact, it's not always the case. Mainstream is even more difficult to break into than ever; especially if you're an unknown author.

It's competitive, and many publishing houses won't even accept submissions unless they're from a literary agent. And trying to find a literary agent who will take on your book is, well, pretty exhausting, too.

That's why, time after time, I will always recommend that authors publish their book on Kindle. There are book-loads of reasons why this is the best option (in my opinion), let me share my top 6 with you.

Publishing on Kindle is the icing on the cake: you've spent HOW long writing this book? And now you're just going to hide it away from the world? Publishing your book on Kindle really is the icing on the cake and the jauntily-placed glace cherry on top. Imagine the feeling when you become a published author. Imagine telling your friends, colleagues and family that you've done it, and you have a real book in your hand to prove it!

You deserve it: the cheerleaders are waiting at the finish line for you, with their pompoms and excited faces. You have come so far; you've worked so hard. You deserve this. Leaving your book unpublished is like travelling halfway across the world for a holiday and then spending a fortnight in your hotel room. You just wouldn't do it, would you?

You call the shots: the Kindle platform has revolutionised the publishing world and it's an opportunity every potential indie author can (and ought to) embrace. As a Kindle author, you hold the reins, you decide how to hatch your book, you don't hand over control of your cover design, word length, price, and everything else – you can boss it any way you like.

The rewards can be huge: you can add "published writer/author" to your portfolio, which will give you kudos amongst your clients (if you've written a biz book). You can draw in a new crowd, perhaps some people who may not have found you via your other marketing platforms. You can make money while you sleep – who wouldn't want easy money like that?

It's free: if you learn how to format your book and upload it to Kindle, you don't have to pay for this exciting adventure, either. There are heaps of YouTube videos out there to teach you how to format your book and upload it to Kindle.

There are stacks of success stories: take a look this Telegraph article http://www.telegraph.co.uk/lifestyle/11789876/Meet-the-Kindlepreneurs.html.

Some of my clients have also enjoyed success – Kate Spencer, for one, https://www.amazon.co.uk/Twelve-Lessons-Kate-Spencer-x/dp/0992710308 - her novels: *Twelve Lessons* and *Twelve Lessons Later* have topped the best-seller charts, too.

How to Make Money by Publishing on Kindle

As a Kindle e-book publisher, I help indie authors' dreams come true. But when my part is over and they're waiting for their royalties to stack up, new authors can get frustrated when their book doesn't bring in what they'd hoped.

Then the tumbleweed starts.

Then the wobbles emerge ("Was my book really any good anyway?").

Then the mind monkeys start screeching ("Nah, it was pretty rubbish really, did you honestly think it was going to be a bestseller?").

Then the confidence wanes and they can't focus on their next writing project because they think they're a failure.

Then they start to believe that they're too amateurish to write any more books. And the vicious cycle continues.

There are ways to avoid this, of course. Here are a few ways to help you steer clear of the deep, dark hole of negativity/fear/insecurity.

Create a series

The more books you have, the more potential you have for all that moola to roll in for the foreseeable. So create a book series of 'How-Tos' and 'FAQs' or a sequel to your novel or a spin-off series. And every time you add another one to the series, add links to it in every one of your other Kindle books and upload them all again.

Share your professional expertise

If you're an expert at something, share your knowledge with a potentially huge global audience and as long as you get all the publishing bits right (as mentioned below), you'll be able to reap all those lovely financial rewards.

Know your target audience inside out and respond to their every pain

Again, if you're an entrepreneur / specialist in something then you should know your ideal customers (and your potential readers) inside out. You should know their pain points and what keeps them awake at 3am. So use this knowledge and write a book that helps them break through all the roadblocks. They'll love you for it AND they'll tell their friends.

Choose your niche

Writing for a niche is much more likely to see your royalties grow because (as in business), you're giving a specific message to a specific audience; instead of using the spray and pray method where you just write and hope someone (anyone) will find it.

Hire a proofreader / copy-editor so that you're confident it's as perfect as it can be

If you're thinking of saving a bit of money by doing your own proofreading / copy-editing, then I would urge you to reconsider. Not only will this be a huge investment (potentially for the long-term success of your book) but it will also lay the foundation for your 'professional indie author' status. I always think it's so sad when I read a book that's full of rich and valuable content, but it's littered with typos and grammatical mistakes.

Market, market, market

Don't just think about marketing in the early days if you want to make REAL money from your Kindle book. Marketing is an ongoing process (just like it is for any kind of business) and it needs to be consistent and continuous. Take every opportunity possible to promote your book, research as much about indie author marketing as you can and this can keep your royalty well from drying up.

Format it beautifully

A beautifully formatted Kindle book is possible. So, take the time to format yours properly and it will give your book even more credibility. Make sure there aren't any broken hyperlinks, that your chapter headings always start on a new page, that you don't have any odd line spacing and that you only use two or three different styles and fonts to keep your book looking professional and uniform.

Get your launch right

Don't just wait until your book is out there before you start talking about it, make sure you build up some excitement too (during the writing process if you can). Tease your potential audience with snippets of book covers, title pages and hints of a foreword from a local celeb/prestigious expert. Make sure they know when the book is coming out or even better, start a VIP pre-order list and you'll be able to count on sales even before the book is finished.

Write a knock-em-dead description that compels readers to buy

As well as peppering your description with hooks and questions and teasers, create a bullet list of reasons why they're going to love your book and include that too. Don't rush this part of your Kindle book publishing process because this is your sales pitch. Get it right and you'll be rewarded, get it wrong and that tumbleweed will start to grow.

Michelle Emerson

How to get your book noticed on Kindle

At the time of writing, there are some 4 million books in the Amazon Kindle Store. It is a list which is comprised of every genre you can imagine and populated by both world famous successful authors to recently self-published writers.

Whether you choose to self-publish on Amazon or hire an e-publisher such as myself to assist you with the process, any established self-published writer will tell you that exposure was vital to their success. The sheer breadth of material available on Amazon Kindle is good news to any writer. It has become a one stop shop for many a reader around the globe and even if you feel daunted by the prospect of trying to launch yourself in a market so flooded with options, you can also rest assured that it is never a market which is saturated. After all, for any reader, there is no such concept as 'too many books'.

The question then is: How as a self-published writer do you get your book noticed in the Kindle Store?

1. Choose the Right Categories - marketing in the Kindle Store relies on your readers finding you quickly and easily. Take time out to consider the genre of your book alongside identifying any applicable sub-categories.

2. Opt into Amazon KDP Select - Amazon's publishing platform is very much geared to aid self-published writers position themselves in the Kindle market. Part of their promotional toolkit is KDP Select. By subscribing to KDP Select you are able to price your book at your desired price point, offer free downloads for a limited period of time and time-limited price discounts. Good news for self-published writers who can gain readership and increase downloads – which, in turn, improves rankings in the Kindle Store! Furthermore, increase exposure by opting into the lending library, and take advantage of the wider global e-book market KDP Select offers. These are time-proven strategies towards building readership which in recent years have served many astute self-published writers well.

3. Add A Smart Link - the benefit of digital publishing is the ability to utilise the perks of internet enabled devices. By adding a smart link to the back of your Kindle book, potential opportunity for 'free' Kindle marketing avails! Make it easy for your readers to share your book on social networks such as Twitter and

Facebook. After all, word of mouth is always the best sales technique.

4. Write A Series - many successful writers on Kindle have done so by understanding that sales and a loyal following often go hand in hand. Exposure can sometimes be gradual, but writing a series opens up the opportunity for increased sales and kudos via current readership loyalty. Don't forget to tantalise your readers with information about up and coming releases in the back of your Kindle Book!

Within my role as an e-publisher many new clients are excited to finally realise that the world of self-publishing has gained momentum. For many, the journey of self-publishing on Kindle is a rewarding experience in itself. The world it is a-changing, and in this respect we need to change our perceptions too. Gone are the times when succeeding as a writer looked nigh on impossible. Take the world by storm and get your book noticed on Kindle!

Printed in Poland
by Amazon Fulfillment
Poland Sp. z o.o., Wrocław